The Power of Play

NEW VISIONS OF CREATIVITY

HOW DO YOU THINK ABOUT PLAY?

PLAYFULLY?

DO YOU TAKE PLAY SERIOUSLY?

DO YOU FIND IT BETTER TO DO THAN TO THINK ABOUT?

ALL OF THE ABOVE?

WELCOME TO THIS CHRYSALIS READER,

WHERE THE SUBJECT IS TAKEN SERIOUSLY,

PLAYED WITH, ANALYZED, INDULGED, IMAGED.

THIS IS A BOOK TO READ FOR FUN

AND PROFIT.

The Power of Play

NEW VISIONS OF CREATIVITY

Edited by Carol S. Lawson

 CHRYSALIS BOOKS

Imprint of the Swedenborg Foundation
West Chester, Pennsylvania

THE CHRYSALIS READER is a book series that examines themes related to the universal quest for wisdom. Inspired by the Swedenborg Foundation journal *Chrysalis,* each volume presents original short stories, essays, poetry, and art exploring the spiritual dimensions of a chosen theme. Works are selected by the series editor. For information on future themes or submission of original writings, contact Carol S. Lawson, Editor, Route 1, Box 184, Dillwyn, Virginia 23936.

© 1996 by the Swedenborg Foundation

Printed on recycled paper and bound in the United States of America

LIBRARY OF CONGRESS CATALOGING-IN-PUBLICATION DATA
The power of play: new visions of creativity
   edited by Carol S. Lawson
      p.   cm.   —(Chrysalis reader: v. 3)
   ISBN 0-87785-227-8
   1. Play—Literary collections. 2. Creative ability—literary collections.
3. American literature—20th century. I. Lawson, Carol S. II. Series.
PS509.P59P69 1996
810.8´0353—dc20
                                                                    96-9648
                                                                    CIP

CHRYSALIS BOOKS
Imprint of the Swedenborg Foundation
320 North Church Street
West Chester, Pennsylvania 19380

Contents

In the Midst of Right Now

To Play
is to meet the divine
in the midst of right now.

To Play
is to move and be still
to laugh
to cry
to dance
and to be surprised
by passion.

To Play
is to discover depths of love,
compassion, justice, and forgiveness.

To Play
is to jump on a rainbow
and swing from cloud to cloud
scattering seedbuds of creativity.

Playfulness

Thus before their eyes all things seem
to laugh and frolic and to live.[1]

—EMANUEL SWEDENBORG

I HAVE A SIX-YEAR-OLD GRANDSON who can hardly walk across a room without falling into some form of play. It is difficult for him to do any task because a neat game intervenes and he forgets the task. To my surprise, the mystic Emanuel Swedenborg describes this situation very well. One is playful when his or her interior state is full of gladness.

> For play is the bodily activity that results from gladness of mind, and all festivity and gladness arise from the delights of the loves an individual possesses. Within play there is also concord, because all interior gladness has harmony in it; if any discord or opposition exists, gladness ceases. Interior gladness is inherent in man's freedom, and all freedom is from love that is not opposed.[2]

This is easily confirmed in my grandson. A scolding or a request for him to do something is a discord that spoils the play. So, when children are at play, they are acting out their feelings of delight, and we might as well just watch and enjoy the process as a reminder that such delight is possible.

One unusual aspect of Swedenborg's work is that he first views things from a heavenly perspective, and this focuses his understanding of what is significant in the everyday world. The following paragraph is an example (Swedenborg is in heaven and is studying how children are instructed there):

> By a method of communication that is familiar in the next life I was shown the nature of young children's ideas when they see

Opposite:
Smiling Figure. Ceramic, 47.5 cm., seventh to ninth century, Veracruz, Mexico. New York: The Metropolitan Museum of Art. The Michael C. Rockefeller Memorial Collection. Bequest of Nelson A. Rockefeller, 1979 (1979.206.1211).

any objects. Their ideas were such that every single thing was living, so that each idea comprising their thought had life within it. I also perceived that the ideas present in young children on earth when playing games were almost the same, for they do not as yet have the ability like adults to reflect on what is inanimate.[3]

And this, too, is easily confirmed. My grandson's plastic Power Rangers talk to him and invite him to play. The world is enlivened by his inner joy.

Of course, there are corresponding states in adults. Long ago I discovered creativity was essentially playing with things. When playing, you aren't concerned with results. Try this and that. See what is the most interesting and the most fun. You simply let yourself do as you feel. For an adult, play can also be taking on a job you just felt like doing at that moment. Rearrange the furniture, do that little thing that has been bothering you for some time. Many successful businesses have simply been the expansion of what someone loved to do.

One of Swedenborg's central ideas is the unique love within an individual's life, which lies hidden at the core of the individual. It is what the person would enjoy doing forever. I just saw on television a young man who had from childhood loved fashion. He dressed up in capes and tassels and would do anything to get a copy of the latest style-setting magazine. He became director of design for *Vogue*. Early on, he was fortunate to sense fashion as the love of his life. Most people have to try many things to find the work that naturally suits them. But, as this style expert says, when you have found it, work is no longer work. Adults feel free when they are doing what they most want to do.

> First, it should be known that all freedom is of love, so much so that love and freedom are one. As love is our life, freedom is our life, too. For every enjoyment is from some love of ours and has no other source, and to act from the enjoyment of one's love is to act in freedom. Enjoyment leads us as the current bears an object along on a stream.[4]

LIFE'S LOVE IS ONE OF THE BIG IDEAS in Swedenborg. It has tremendous implications as to where one can find pleasure. It transcends ordinary concepts of aptitude. Each one's love-of-his-life is unique to eternity. It is the inward way the individual can develop most easily and delightfully. Just as in heaven children are first shown deeper things in the midst of their games, we too are guided when we follow what is within us.

Finally Swedenborg describes what happens when individuals follow the drift of their unique life's love. The way opens up into the universal where they find themselves in accord with the total design of existence. It is there that "before their eyes all things seem to laugh and frolic and to live." Because the individual is fully expressing what is within, the world he or she experiences is enlivened. The play of both the child and the adult fully enjoying their powers is a similar process, only at a higher level of understanding in the adult. It is play either way. Indeed in Hinduism the ultimate nature of existence is said to be *lila,* play. Often people are shocked when they first hear of this. They had expected something more serious and ponderous. But it was the mystics who had made the great journey described in the *Upanishads* who came back with this news: It is all play. The world was and is created playfully.

WILSON VAN DUSEN is a retired clinical psychologist, a Swedenborg scholar, and author. He says he is the only mystic who rides a motorcycle.

Notes

In Swedenborgian studies it is customary to reference a particular text by the book's title and Swedenborg's paragraph number, as the numbers are uniform in all editions. The translations in this preface have been slightly altered to accord with contemporary language.

1. Emanuel Swedenborg. *Heaven and Hell.* Paragraph no. 489.
2. ———. *Arcana Coelestia.* Paragraph no. 10416.
3. Ibid. Paragraph no. 2298.
4. Emanuel Swedenborg. *Divine Providence.* Paragraph no. 73.

The Power of Play

NEW VISIONS OF CREATIVITY

PART I

Risk-taking

THE PLAYERS:

Luke Skywalker of *The Empire Strikes Back*
Yoda, an other-worldly guru

As the scene opens, Yoda is teaching Luke
to do something he plainly considers impossible.

LUKE: I'll try.
YODA: [scornfully] There is no 'try'. Either 'do' or 'not do'.

Yoda voices a familiar aspect of contemporary
success-seeking culture. These pages of The Power
of Play *reveal this all-American, go-get'm attitude*
to be a contemporary example of that old Aristotelian
bugaboo, the Fallacy of the Excluded Middle. 'Try'
may not be the middle term between the poles of 'do'
and 'not do', but 'play' certainly is. Some of the mean-
ings we assign to 'play' provide a viable alternative
between trying and doing, an alternative compatible
with, and distinguishable from, both of them.

A creative approach to a complex problem is
to "play with it for a while." The risk involved
in play is more acceptable than "real" failure
and is a risk that can be instructive, informative,
encouraging, inspiring.

The Creative
is A Precious
Vital Force
that must be
Cared for
and Loved.

KATE CHENEY CHAPPELL
AND ADDISON CASTLE ULRICH

Turtle Song, Heron Dance

Come with me, for a little while.
Listen to the song of the turtle.
See the dance of the heron.

—KATE RANSOHOFF

I

CHAPPELL: On the first floor of the Charles River Studio Workshop grown-ups play—sometimes alone, sometimes together—with every sort of odds and ends (sticks, buttons, shells, fabric, huge cylinders, and tiny seeds) imaginable. The Studio is like a giant kindergarten for adults, and yet the work we do there embodies a philosophy as old as the beginnings of recorded civilization and captures the shared essence of ancient religions. As Kate Ransohoff the Studio's director says, "Art results from an active encounter between a human being and 'an other' whether that other is called nature, God, psyche, culture, or community."

To help these encounters—this art—to happen, the Studio has created a physical environment where play can take place in an atmosphere of trust. Permission is given to experiment freely, to push our limits instead of worrying about a finished product. The emphasis is on the process of play and the supportive environment allows the Studio's credo to be realized: *In play the natural connective tissues of body and soul function as one; therein is the power of play.* And, therein, of course, the individual meets his own spark of the divine, the power within the imagination.

Opposite:
Kate Ransohoff.
Untitled. Ink on rice
paper, 1996.

Studio attendees are artists who work in various media. When our Studio works are completed, we gather and talk to the group about what it is we have made there and what it means to us. There is a sense of community that allows play to happen freely. Everyone is on an equal footing. There are "coaches" instead of teachers, who are friends and fellow artists, who are advocates for the creative process and your companions for the journey. The coach's job is to listen to you when you are ready to process your work, describe what you say, and hand the work back to you. Respectful silence can be a provocative and empowering response. It has allowed me to discover my own truth and to evolve my own artwork rather than to respond and adapt to external cues.

As a professional artist, I came here to find a new direction in my work. After balancing a twenty-two-year business partnership with my husband against a painting career on the side, I decided to put art first. At the same time, I was growing in spiritual ways, connecting to a creative force that I sensed both in nature and myself. The artwork I was making sometimes sprang from that spiritual center in me, and I wanted more of that connection.

I thus came ready for serious work but found I was not so prepared for serious play. The program at CRSW begins with the premise that play is essential to the creative process. Being brought up in traditional schools and colleges that emphasize an academic approach to art, I never had a course called "Play!" Now I was being asked to let go of the old rules and look to my own intuition as my seat of authority.

The play process amazed me. My rational mind found it hard to believe that an inaccessible playful part of me could hold truth, too. Often play at the Studio resulted in a revelation of something about me—my feelings, my longings, my dreams—and my visions would suddenly take shape. The odd arrangement of objects had embodied some hitherto hidden part of me.

II

ULRICH: Founder and director of CRSW, Kate Ransohoff describes the nature of play as a way for people to access their latent creative abilities. She says that the need to create is based on the primary impulse to make things and to make sense of life's events. The things we make can be ideas, inventions, forms of art, or scientific theories. They can be shaped from wrestling with a question, observation, or dilemma, and materials which can be pushed around and brought into shape.

To look at work, to
make work, to put it
in our houses is to
connect with how we
feel about nature,
about faith, about
human beings, about
what we are doing here,
and how we would like
life to be cared for,
and how we feel
when it is not.

Kate Ransohoff.
Untitled. Ink on rice
paper, 1996.

Kate Ransohoff told me she had been fortunate in encountering
teachers who provided space and modalities for her own creative energy. She described the dance studio of Ruth St. Denis, for example,
where as a young dancer she learned that discrete elements—story-
telling, theater, costume, music, movement, space, imagination, and
passion could transform a small detail of life into a remembrance—
an affecting image, a dance—that which is called art. With the birth
of her children Kate ceased being a dance performer. Someone gave
her some mahogany and woodworking tools, and she found another medium that began to satisfy her creative impulse. She became in-

terested in the visual arts. She wrestled with aesthetic principles and hierarchies and categories of art and instinctively recoiled from all notions of artistic exclusivity. She began to see that being creative has become a privilege for those who are called gifted, talented, or genius, and that thereby we have deprived great numbers of people in work, in schools, in families from being as productive, as alive, as filled with a sense of competence, as they might be. What began to emerge in Ransohoff's consciousness, she says, was an appreciation for diversity, the perennial values in the traditional arts, and the importance of play, practice, and space as preconditions for making art.

III

CHAPPELL: What has happened to my own work since I started to play? It literally jumped off the wall. At the beginning of my time at the Charles River Studio Workshop, I had an experience which grabbed me by the shoulders and shook my old assumptions to the core. I was attracted to a nine-foot-long roll of black photographic paper. I unrolled a portion and tacked it up on the wall to do a painting, but I started by making a tear in the black paper. From the hole came rays of color. The torn black bits became like tongues. They curved over, and I painted them too. I made chalk marks—islands or cells—blue surrounded by red, red surrounded by blue, purple spheres with twisting blue or red threads with a lot of motion. I put the yellow paint on last—sparks of light like phosphorescence of plankton, wiggly life-like forms.

Then a wonderful thing happened that, for me, was like discovering the world wasn't flat anymore. I pulled the painting down and noticed that it wanted to roll up and stand by itself. I was really excited! The negative space was a deeper black than the paper. I had always thought of myself as a painter, but now the three-dimensional world of sculpture jumped off the wall and into my life. From that first cylinder, I went on to make a cluster of black rolled free-standing "paintings." I began to think about creation itself and the connections between the life of a cell and the spinning universe. Since then, I have continued to explore origins, life springing from darkness and the deep. I see the interplay of all forms of life in the things I make, from single-cell protozoa to the huge leviathan. In their interdependency I am reminded that the sea cradles humankind as well, and that our vitality depends on this fragile eco-system.

This active encounter exemplifies what the Studio's environment is designed for: connecting elements of ourselves with elements of the universe. It is in play that one is able to open to the possible encounter, and to open to the diverse elements that may facilitate or make up the encounter. Play leads one out of the social rigidities, stereotypes, and biases with which the individual protects the self from becoming subsumed and losing control. Importance temporarily shifts from the finished piece of art to the ongoing process of creativity itself. In the shifts and recombinations of play, the player opens the self to contact with the divine, the other, and the universe.

Something else happened to me at the Studio. I have begun to write poetry again after a twenty-year hiatus, and the poetry I write often connects with the art I am making. I am encouraged by this dialogue of two forms of expressions, which I used to think had to be separate.

In Mircea Eliades's *Cosmos and History: The Myth of the Eternal Return,* he talks about the lunar myth which sees the disappearance of the moon (three days of darkness) as a necessary death before its reappearance. I have experienced a death in many of my old attitudes and beliefs about art, about myself, about God and Spirit. Old forms are giving way to new ones, and part of the art-making for me has been a search for what Eliade calls the *"undivided one* of precreation."

I am still in transition with my work, and some days I long to go back to my old routines. Back then I thought that my creativity, like many things in my life, was in limited supply. I imagined it was a well, and that if I went to the well too many times, I would run dry. Now I experience this well as the limitless spring of God's love. If I play at its edge, I fall into waters that bring me insight and images and strength.

As adults, work is what we know. I have a new way of looking at both work and play, thanks to my experience at CRSW, work and play are not opposites; they are part of the same process. Play is an *essential activity of the creative self at work.* The nature of the artist's work balances play—a kind of child's intense, focused absorption in imaginary worlds—with the disciplined practice of the adult's hands and mind. Play was a valuable key to my recovering spontaneity and joy and the feel of the sacred in my work.

According to Kate Ransohoff, the Hebrew word to "work" and "worship" come from the same root: to labor for something is to honor it. There is honor and worshipfulness as well as laughter and smiles in the act of play.

KATE CHENEY CHAPPELL is a painter who has studied at l'Atelier Goetz in Paris, the University of Southern Maine, Charles River Studio Workshop in Massachusetts, and Haystack Mountain School in Maine. ADDISON CASTLE ULRICH has worked with Kate Ransohoff in a new art making studio in Alexandria, Virginia. She is a freelance writer and a scholar of Indian art.

Somewhere Else

WHILE MY MOTHER WAS DYING, I developed a great urge to go out and do things I'd never done before, things I'd always wanted to do, or maybe something that had just occurred to me when leafing through the pages of a *National Geographic* while waiting for Dr. Dwightman to finish Mrs. Abbott's crown. I'd guess that this is a common occurrence among middle-aged children, poised at the final orphaning. It is, in any event, how I ended up in Nepal, a tiny speck under the towering Himalayas. I went there, I think, just to find out if I was still alive.

It was all a lark at first. I only had to carry a minuscule day pack with camera and snacks, my water bottles, and my down jacket. Yaks carried all the substantial items of food, clothing, and tents. Without a heavy pack, I reasoned, I could walk anywhere. I was in good shape for a woman my age, and I trained well, as much as you can train to climb over 18,000 foot passes on the bumps of Vermont hills which rise a mere 1,500 feet into the clouds. On these training runs, I imagined the beautiful photographs I'd take to impress my married friends whose babies kept them house-bound and sleep deprived. Isn't that what the single life is all about? To go where you want, when you want, to stay as long as you like, always free to move on?

The mountains were so demanding. I couldn't walk among them and think about being anywhere else. I loved the mystical silence of the river valleys, the flocks of circling snow pigeons, their underbellies silver against the deep dustless blue sky. I was transported by the monks chanting, beating their drums and ringing bells, blowing conch horns from their lonely mountaintop monastery.

Opposite: Nicholas Roerich. *The Master's Command,* detail. Tempera on canvas, 60¼×33 inches, 1947. Bangalore, India: Svetoslav Roerich Collection.

I rejoiced with every step that took me farther away from home, leaving behind the weight of the dying and forging lightly ahead into the unknown. Every day was what it was, an unfolding of light and dreams. I became a human walking machine, sucking in oxygen and pumping out CO_2. I was invincible. I roared up the hillsides, flew over the ridges, stopping only long enough to veer off in another direction to climb everything in sight.

So it was a surprise, really, when I got sick. It started off innocuously enough. A scratchy throat. A light cold. Despite Vitamin C and saltwater gargles, it got worse. As we climbed higher, every night camping 2,000 feet above where we slept the night before, the temperature dropped accordingly. It looked the same. There wasn't any snow on the ground, and only my water bottle froze overnight, if I didn't put it in the bottom of my sleeping bag with my boots. It was getting crowded in that sleeping bag, and I started having trouble sleeping.

My head was so full, I couldn't breathe except through my mouth, and when I lie down and try to relax, I only think about how badly I need to get up and go pee. An ordeal. I untied my mummy hood, unzipped my bag, crawled out of it, and wiggled out of the liner that would come out with me. I dug out my boots and laced them up, crawled to the door on my hands and knees, unzipped the tent, unzipped the vestibule, and, like a butterfly, emerged into the eerie green moonlight that transformed every boulder into some twisted titan or demented gnome. It was freezing out, and a little scary, as if I had awakened in someone else's nightmare. Then I would slug down another quart of water, for I was always thirsty, and reverse the procedure.

For a few nights I got up eight or nine times, toward morning snatching maybe fifteen minutes of sleep in between. Suddenly it would be time to get up and face the day. And at last I could breathe again.

The landscape was stunning. I have beautiful pictures. I can show you. And there were those moments of transcendence when for whole minutes I did not wish with every fiber of my being to be somewhere else. I watched the choughs fold their wings and drop like stones through the sky in front of Everest. I watched the full moon set in the Evening-in-Paris-blue sky at daybreak over the sentinel cliffs of the Cho La.

There were those unforgettable crucibles too, icy ones. Losing my mitten in the icefields at the top of the pass, I retraced my boot prints in the snow over and over until I had to go on without it. The rest of the long day was spent with the fingers of one hand slowly going numb, then mittening that hand up, and letting my warm set of fingers turn cold.

Somehow, I ended up on a winter camping trip. All I thought about was getting warm and staying warm or burying myself deep within my sleeping bag.

One morning I crawled out of my tent to find everything covered in hoar frost—the prayer flags, the tent ropes, the rocks, and weeds. Even the yaks, their breath steaming the air, were covered in a blanket of ice crystals. It was as if the Snow Queen herself had come during the night. I looked around to see if costumed figures were about to dance a *pas de deux* for my benefit. But there was only me, shivering alone with cold hands and feet in front of my tent somewhere in Nepal.

And that was the moment I knew I was alive. Because when you're alive, your feet get cold, you can't sleep, and things don't go according to plan. When you're alive, you wake up to find all the ordinary things shining in crystalline splendor in a way you never saw them before.

LANI WRIGHT's home base is in Vermont.

Leah Olivier.
Lost Mitten.
Pencil, 1996.

RAYMOND WONG

The Monkey
A Buddhist Myth

Head of Hanuman,
detail. Indonesian. Terra
cotta, 4¾×9¾×9¾
inches, ca. fourteenth
century. Los Angeles
County Museum of Art.
Gift of Marilyn Walter
Grounds (M.86.346.1).
This simian head proba-
bly belongs to an image
of the monkey-god
Hanuman.

LIN YU VILLAGE STIRRED IN EXCITEMENT. "The Emperor is coming!" the villagers whispered to one another. Hidden in a wooded valley in northern China, the small village of some thirty peasant families had never experienced such a thrilling event.

"Mamma, who is the Emperor?" asked Bao-bao, a little boy sitting on a small clay bed. He was holding a live monkey.

"The Son of Heaven!" said his mother, heating some *jook* [rice gruel] in an iron pot on top of a brick stove. The one-room hut was sparsely furnished. Here Bao-bao was born ten years ago; also in this room his father had died of tuberculosis.

"Is he God?" asked the boy.

"No. But he controls everything and everyone under the sky," said the mother. "They say he lives in a palace in Peking with three thousand rooms and ten thousand servants. But now the Emperor and his royal guards are on a hunting trip, and they will stop over here tomorrow night."

"Where is he going to sleep?"

"In the temple. Come, eat some jook, then feed the pigs. Then we will go to the temple to help out. We will get to see the Emperor!"

"Can I bring Tartar with me, Mamma?"

"No! Come, eat your jook before it gets cold." The woman poured out some steaming gruel and placed a pair of chopsticks on the table. The boy slipped off the bed with the monkey on his back.

Before eating, he fed the monkey out of his bowl. Watching him, his mother shook her head in disapproval.

To everyone in the village, the monkey had long been a mystery. On a stormy summer night at the precise moment Bao-bao was born, a dark shadow appeared on the yellow rice-paper window pane. As the newborn baby let out his first cry, a blast of wind blew open the window, revealing a monkey squatting on the window ledge. Everyone in the room was stunned. Never before had a monkey been sighted in the village or the nearby woods. After the initial shock, they tried to chase the creature out of the hut. Instead, it jumped onto the clay bunk. Screaming, the mother shielded her squalling newborn. But no harm came. Swinging its tail, the monkey hopped around; then it cradled its arms like a mother rocking a baby to sleep. Surprisingly, little Bao-bao, his eyes not yet open, slowly turned his head toward the monkey and stopped crying. He even opened his little mouth and seemed to be smiling. From that moment on, the monkey became part of the family. They called it Tartar.

After feeding the pigs, Bao-bao and his mother left for the temple on top of a hill overlooking the valley. The village chief, an elderly man with high cheekbones, thick eyebrows, and a long beard, was directing the cleaning and decorating for the one-night stay of the Emperor and his royal entourage. All the villagers, except the feeble, scrubbed the brick floors, washed the windows, cleaned the walls, and polished the red wooden columns standing on either side of a golden clay Buddha. The village chief, acting like an emperor himself, supervised every detail of the preparation until long after dark. Tired and hungry, Bao-bao and his mother followed a moonlit trail through the rice paddies to their simple hut.

SHORTLY AFTER DAWN THE FOLLOWING MORNING, Bao-bao's mother motioned him to come to the doorway. The hut fronted on a narrow cobblestone street, the main passageway through the village. Early as it was on this chilly autumn morning, excited crowds had gathered. An advance unit of thirty royal guards on white horses had arrived. The guards wore black silk hats with bright yellow bands pleated around the rims, blue jackets with red sashes, and silver shields displaying the royal golden dragon. The village chief and several elders greeted the new arrivals. Soon a team of coolies arrived, followed by more royal guards. On their backs they carried heavy loads of equipment, including the emperor's bed. Bowing to the captain of the guards, the village chief led the way to the temple.

More imperial retinue arrived—the chamberlain, the royal household staff, and the chef and his assistants. A kitchen was set up in the temple; the entire village was invited to a feast that night. The village chief assigned villagers to different tasks—chopping wood, setting up tables, washing rice, and cutting vegetables.

The Son of Heaven descended to Lin Yu Village in an enclosed sedan chair. The bearers shouldering the right and left poles wore sleeveless blue jackets with a white symbol of the royal dynasty sewed on front. Everyone knelt and kowtowed on the roadside as the gold and yellow chair escorted by mounted soldiers passed by.

Bao-bao, his mother, and the rest of the village workers left the temple before sunset to get ready for the feast. Back in the village, unpleasant news was waiting.

"They took your pigs!" shouted an old man to Bao-bao's mother. He had been spared the chores at the temple because of his age.

"What are you talking about? Who took my pigs?" she asked.

"The soldiers!"

Not believing what she heard, Bao-bao's mother rushed back to the hut, pushed open the bamboo pig sty and looked inside. Her pigs were gone, all four of them. While she stood staring at the empty pig pen, her next-door neighbor came. "They grabbed our chickens!" said the woman. "Not only that, they beat up Lao Chu and took all his corn."

"Mamma! Where is Tartar?" Bao-bao yelled.

"I don't know, he must be around somewhere," said the mother, irritated by the interruption.

"I can't find him! I looked everywhere!" shouted the boy. Running out to the street, he asked a group of villagers if any one had seen the monkey. They looked at him; one was on the verge of saying something but was hushed by the others.

"Come back here! It's time to get dressed for the feast," shouted Bao-bao's mother from the hut's doorway. When Bao-bao, still looking for his pet, did not respond, she came out and forced him back to the hut. "I want my Tartar!" cried the little boy.

"Stop crying! Tartar has gone to the woods before; he always comes back," said his mother.

On their way to the temple, Bao-bao and his mother met more villagers, all dressed in their best. The narrow dirt road stretched through the empty field, and the late autumn sun was setting. A flight of stone stairs, lit on both sides with strings of red lanterns, led to the temple gate. Inside, the villagers gathered in groups, some talking among themselves, others walking around admiring the colorful decorations. A long strip of red carpet with embroidered gold dragons covered the path between the makeshift royal chamber and the main hall where the feast was to be served.

A gong was sounded. The chamber door slowly opened, and the Emperor stepped out, followed by royal escorts. The village chief ordered everyone to kneel and bow. No one dared look up or make the slightest noise as the Emperor majestically walked across the carpeted path. Only after the Emperor had been seated in a high teakwood chair on the altar in front of the giant golden Buddha were the villagers admitted into the dining hall. They arrived in single file, led by the village chief, dressed in a black silk gown and a blue silk vest.

"Long live your Majesty! Ten thousand years!" shouted the village chief. The other villagers followed him, chanting the same in unison. The Emperor beamed a benign smile and gestured for them to sit down. The feast began. Steaming barbecued pigs and chickens, shark-fin soup, stir-fried noodles and vegetables, hot buns seasoned with spicy sauce, corn cakes, and sweet potatoes were served in large trays and beautiful porcelain bowls by the court attendants. The villagers enjoyed the festivity and the royal treatment, and, being peasant folk, they were overcome by the presence of the Son of Heaven. They talked in low voices and refrained from excessive drinking.

A sudden silence gripped the air as the chef himself, assisted by several kitchen hands, brought out the last course: a live monkey! The animal was clamped around the neck against an iron rod attached to a barbecue pit on wheels. The monkey was to be slowly roasted to death. The chef would then crack open its head and scoop out the brain as a nourishing delicacy. They said it would make a person strong and smart. Before lighting the charcoal, the chef paraded the doomed animal in front of the Emperor to show that it was alive. The villagers held their breath. They had heard of this, but none had dreamed of seeing it happen before their eyes.

Just as the chef was about to light the charcoal, a sudden piercing scream broke the silence: "Tartar!" Springing up from his seat, a terrified boy dashed across the hall to the altar. Bao-bao threw himself upon the barbecue cart, overturning it and scattering the charcoal over the red carpet. The iron rod of the barbecue pit smashed against the ground and the clamps burst open. The monkey jumped into the boy's arms, and before anyone realized what was happening, Bao-bao had run out of the hall with the monkey.

"Stop him!" shouted the guards.

"Please don't hurt him! He is my son!" yelled Bao-bao's mother.

Shaken, the village chief knelt in front of the altar kowtowing and begging His Majesty for forgiveness. The Emperor waved his hand, dismissing him. Then, turning to the royal guards, he ordered the captain to bring the boy back, unharmed. "And the monkey too, dead or alive," he added.

Two imperial guards, armed with swords, each carrying a bow and a bag of arrows on his back, marched out of the hall on the double with the captain. By then, leaping over several steps at a time,

Bao-bao had already reached the bottom of the stairway. He ran across the dirt path, through the field, and into the woods while his pursuers chased after him, yelling for him to stop. As soon as he reached the first cluster of tall aspen trees, he let go of the monkey. "Run, Tartar, run! Don't come back!" he shouted, tears streaming down his cheeks. The monkey leaped to the top of the tree and looked down at Bao-bao. "Good-bye, Tartar! Run!" again shouted Bao-bao. Within seconds, one royal guard grabbed Bao-bao by the arm; the other pointed at the top of the tree. "There's the monkey!"

Struggling, Bao-bao kicked at the tree trunk. "Run!" he shouted. This time the monkey fled, leaping from one treetop to another until it had reached the foot of a rocky hill some distance away. There it stopped. Dragging Bao-bao along with them, the captain and the two guards hastened their pursuit.

"Shoot!" ordered the captain as soon as they were within range of their target. Quickly the guards took their stance and drew the arrows aiming at the monkey. Bao-bao sprang up and plunged on the guards, knocking them out of position. The arrows missed the target and hit a rock. Suddenly there was a blinding flash of light. The monkey disappeared and the rock split open like a cave. Terrified, the guards stepped backward, ready to flee.

"Do not move!" ordered the captain.

"Let us get away from here, sir," pleaded one of the guards, still holding the bow in his hand.

"Be quiet!" whispered the captain. "I see light in the cave."

Suddenly they heard a distant voice calling "Bao-bao . . ."

Bao-bao . . . Bao-bao, the surrounding hills echoed with the call. Everybody stood still. The voice came from the direction of the cave. "Come, Bao-bao," it said, "bring the captain and the soldiers with you. I want to talk to them."

The guards looked at the captain; the captain stared at the boy. "Who's Bao-bao? Is it you?" asked the captain. Bao-bao nodded, a little frightened himself.

"Don't be afraid, Bao-bao, I am your friend. Tell the others no harm will come to them; I have a message for the Emperor," the voice reverberated in the woods. For a moment, Bao-bao stood there staring at the faint glimmer from the cave. Then, turning to the captain, he asked, "Are you coming, sir?"

"Where to?"

"That cave. Someone is waiting for us."

The captain hesitated. The guards shook their heads.

"I'll go by myself then," said Bao-bao.

"Wait, we'll go with you," the captain responded after a pause. He ordered the two guards to follow him.

It was dark. Somewhere in the woods an owl hooted—*whoo, whoo, whoo, whoo-ah.* Led by the boy, the captain and the guards followed a narrow path winding through the thick clusters of trees. No one talked; the only sound they made were their own footsteps thrashing on fallen leaves. Approaching the cave, they slowed down. Cautiously they inched forward and one by one entered the cave.

"Come in, Bao-bao," a voice thundered from inside. Suddenly the entranceway lightened.

As they turned the corner, they all froze at what they saw—a strange creature sitting on top of a rock, with long furry arms and legs but with the snow-white hair, bushy eyebrows, and long beard of a human. Instinctively the guards reached for their bows and arrows. At that very instant, a piercing beam of light shot out from the creature's eyes, turning the weapons into flames and throwing the guards backward. Frightened and bewildered, the captain and his soldiers huddled together on the ground, speechless. Bao-bao was more curious than scared. He ventured a few steps toward the creature and asked, "Are you . . . are you . . . Tartar?"

"Yes, Bao-bao, I am," said the monkey-man in a kind voice.

"What has become of you?"

"I may look different, but I am still your Tartar," said the strange looking creature. "I was sent here to guide and protect you by Lord Kwan Kung. I disguised myself as a monkey so that I could be your pet and be close to you."

"Who's Lord Kwan Kung?"

"He rules another world far, far away in the heavens. You were a prince in your previous life, and Lord Kwan Kung was your father."

"Do they all look like you in the other world?"

"Yes. But we can change into any form we wish, and we fight evil everywhere. You are destined to do great things—bring food to the hungry, bring hope to the downtrodden, bring justice to all citizens of the Middle Kingdom."

"How could I?" asked Bao-bao. "I am just a poor peasant boy."

"Your destiny is written in the stars; no one but you yourself can change it. The stars shine at night when all is dark; you too will rise and shine from a humble start. Now, let me talk to the captain."

Waving his arm, Tartar, the monkey-man, motioned the captain to step forward. "Come, listen. I will not harm you," said Tartar.

Slowly the captain and the guards rose from their knees. Nervously they looked at Bao-bao.

"Don't be afraid; he is my friend," said the boy.

As they approached the rock where Tartar was sitting, the light vanished. "Ai yeeah!" one guard screamed, drawing echoes from the surrounding walls. It was so dark, they could not see one another. Then the bearded human face of Tartar encircled by a halo appeared.

"Soldiers of the Emperor! I summon you in the name of the mighty Lord Kwan Kung. You are entrusted with a noble mission," proclaimed Tartar. "Your Emperor is a good man, but he is surrounded by corrupt eunuchs. The people of the Middle Kingdom have been suffering too long from famine, disease, and unbearable taxes. Tell your Emperor to take this boy to Peking. Send him to the best schools. He will grow to be the wisest scholar and the bravest warrior and will help the Emperor govern the country in time of peace, defend the country in time of war, and improve the lot of the common people. See that no harm comes to him, or great harm will come to you and your Emperor. Now, go! I will be watching."

"Where will you be, Tartar?" asked Bao-bao.

"I will never be far from you, but I can no longer be your pet. I will protect you and guide you. When you need me, just close your eyes and whisper 'Tartar'. I will be there. Go now to the Emperor with the captain; you have a long journey ahead." With these parting words, Tartar faded out of sight, and the cave brightened. Like waking up from a dream, Bao-bao looked around and met the eyes of the captain and the guards. He felt older and stronger. Looking one last time at the spot where Tartar had been, he led the way out. The cave disappeared, and the rock resumed its original shape.

Crossing the open field, they heard cymbals, drums, string, and other percussion instruments. The royal court musicians were entertaining the Emperor and the villagers, while awaiting the return of the boy, the monkey, and their captors. When Bao-bao entered the great hall of the temple, the music stopped and everyone looked in their direction. Halfway to the altar, Bao-bao's mother ran out and held the boy in her arms. "What have you done, son?" she asked in terror. "Don't worry, Mamma, I will be all right," said Bao-bao as he gently freed himself from her hold and proceeded with the others to the altar. They all knelt and kowtowed to the Emperor.

"Where is the monkey?" asked the Emperor.

"Your Majesty, it . . . it is not a monkey," stuttered the captain.

"Not a monkey? What do you mean?"

The captain was so nervous, he looked at Bao-bao.

"Speak up, boy!" ordered the Son of Heaven.

Unlike the captain, Bao-bao was not intimidated. He raised his head and looked the Emperor squarely in the eye. "His name is Tartar," said the boy in a clear voice.

"Tartar? Who is Tartar?" asked the Emperor.

"The monkey you were trying to kill. He is my friend. He is a god from another world."

"What is he talking about?" the Emperor asked the captain.

"It is the truth, your Majesty," said the captain. "That monkey split open a large rock at the foot of the mountain with a flash of lightning, and he turned into a creature half-man, half-monkey. He said he is from another world, and he told me to tell your Majesty to take this boy with you to the palace in Peking."

"What for? So that he can spoil some more of my parties?" interrupted the Emperor.

"No, your Majesty. The monkey-god said that when the boy is of age he will serve you well against all enemies and bring prosperity to the common people."

The Emperor frowned. "I commanded you to bring back the monkey, and you disobeyed my order. Do you really think you can fool me with all this nonsense? I hereby order you beheaded!"

At a signal from the head eunuch who stood behind the Emperor, several royal guards stepped forward and grabbed the condemned officer by the arms.

At that instant, a sudden gust of wind roared through the hall, blowing out the light in all the lanterns. The villagers screamed. In the midst of the terror and chaos, Tartar, the monkey-man, appeared. "Silence!" he ordered aloud. Turning to the Emperor, he said, "Take this boy with you to your palace; educate him, and train him. Someday you will be glad you did."

The Emperor stared at the creature, trying to remain calm. "What will I need him for? He's just a peasant boy," he said.

"He is not just a peasant boy. If you are the Son of Heaven, he is the lightning rod between heaven and earth. For too long you have been surrounded by conniving eunuchs and corrupt officials who suppress the people and impoverish the land in your name. This boy is destined to help you to change all that."

Hearing this, the head eunuch abruptly stepped forward and knelt before the Emperor. "I beg your Majesty not to believe a word this . . . this creature said. This is sorcery! I have always served you faithfully, and I always will. Let me get rid of them. Soon it will be

Tung Ch'i–ch'ang. *Chien River, Landscape.* Chinese hanging scroll, ink and light color on paper, 24½×49½ inches, Ming Dynasty, ca. 1620. New Haven: Yale University Art Gallery. Gift of Leonard C. Hanna Jr., B.A. 1913 and Mrs. Paul Moore, and Anonymous Oriental Purchase Funds.

dawn, and I will behead the captain as you have ordered. He disobeyed you and brought all these evils here."

The Emperor hesitated. Taking that as a sign of consent, the head eunuch ordered the guards to seize the boy and shoot the monkey-man. He also ordered immediate execution of the captain who was dragged away by the guards. Bao-bao was next. Just then, the monkey-man disappeared. In its place was a large, fierce tiger, its dull yellow fur striped with black. The tiger let out a thunderous roar. The villagers screamed. The guards dropped their bows and arrows and scattered. The Emperor was so terrified, he leaned backward, overturning his chair, and fell on the floor. The head eunuch crawled underneath the table. Bao-bao was the only one who remained calm. He sensed that the tiger was Tartar in disguise. While everyone else was stricken with fear, Bao-bao walked over to the fierce-looking animal and patted it on the head. "Are you Tartar?" he whispered into the tiger's ear. The tiger gently rubbed its face on Bao-bao's chest and sat back on its hind legs. Everybody watched in disbelief. When the Emperor rose from the floor, one of the royal guards quickly restored the chair to its place. The Emperor sat and ordered the boy to come.

"Are you the son of the devil?" asked the Emperor.

"I am the son of my mother; she is not a devil!" said Bao-bao.

"Tell me then, who am I?"

"The Son of Heaven, Emperor of the Middle Kingdom."

"Should everyone be loyal to me?"

"Loyalty can only come from the heart, not from fear."

"Will you be loyal to me?"

"Yes, if you care for the people and protect our country."

"Which is our longest river?"

"The Yellow River."

"What is the name of the highest mountain of this land?"

"Tien Shan."

"Will I reign for ten thousand years?"

"They call you the Son of Heaven; but still, you are a mortal. No mortal can live that long. You can leave a legacy that will last more than ten thousand years."

"Am I almighty?"

"You are not invincible as your eunuchs and generals would like you to believe. The Mongols are lurking in the deserts outside the Great Wall, waiting for the right moment to attack and conquer the Middle Kingdom."

"You are a strange boy, so young yet so smart. You are the first person to be so honest with me. I think I like you. Will you come with me to Peking?"

"If I can bring my mother and Tartar with me."

While the Emperor was talking to Bao-bao, the head eunuch sneaked out of the room. He returned shortly, holding a large silver tray with both hands; on it was a human head soaked in blood! It was the head of the captain! The villagers screamed and moaned in terror, many covering their eyes with their hands.

"As your Majesty has ordered, the captain has been put to death," pronounced the eunuch, kneeling and holding the tray in front of his chest. The Emperor turned his head, looking away from the bloody tray and waving his hand in repulsion. "Take it away!" he ordered. Suddenly, the mutilated head on the tray turned into a serpent. Flickering its long forked tongue, the black and orange striped reptile flipped onto the floor. The eunuch screamed, throwing the tray into the air. Before he could get up from his knees, the snake raised its head and struck. It coiled around the man's trembling body, squeezing tighter and tighter until his torso went limp. Then, with one bite on the throat, the eunuch was dead. It all happened so quickly, everyone froze in silence and fright. Somewhere outside, a rooster crowed. It was almost dawn.

The Emperor broke the silence. "I came here to hunt, and I am richly rewarded, not with trophies, but with a timely message: I must rule wisely and justly, or there will be trouble across this land," proclaimed the Son of Heaven. "Hear me, you people, I will wipe out corruption in the palace and put the right people in the right places to help me govern. Where there is famine, there will be food; where there is flood, a dam will be built; where there is drought, I will pray to Heaven for rain. I will reduce taxes; your labor and sweat will be justly rewarded. To you the soldiers, be on the alert for lurking barbarians. Defend your country! Protect the people! Your bravery and loyalty will be honored and will live on for ten thousand years."

The villagers listened while the Emperor spoke. The serpent lay heaped, motionless, in coils next to the body of the eunuch. The tiger disappeared. Once again, Tartar revealed himself in true form before the Emperor—a monkey with the head and face of a man.

"Well said, great Emperor! May your will be strong and the fair wind be with you," said Tartar. "Take good care of Bao-bao. Educate and train him in his growing years; prepare him for his calling when he is of age; trust him to serve you and the people in time of peace and to defend the country in time of war."

"Tartar, are you not coming with us?" asked Bao-bao.

"No, Bao-bao, I must return to Lord Kwan Kung. He is waiting for my report on my mission. Remember what I told you: if you need me, just close your eyes and call Tartar, and I will be there," said the monkey-man. Turning to the serpent, he ordered, "Be gone, captain! You were born in the Year of the Serpent; to your origin you have returned. When the moon is full on the fifteenth day of the first month twelve lunar years from now, you will be reborn to a family in Tibet; and you will grow up to be a monk. Now go! You are free." Instantly the serpent disappeared. Tartar, too was gone. Two royal guards removed the body of the eunuch, and the Emperor retreated to the rear chamber. The villagers left the temple as dawn glimmered.

The road to Peking was long and winding; the royal hunting party decided to have an early start. By midday, after only a few hours' rest, the Emperor and his entourage were ready to depart. Led by the village chief, the villagers lined the narrow dirt road to bid the Son of Heaven a safe journey home. "Long live your Majesty! Ten thousand years!" they chanted as the procession of gold-colored sedan chairs, horse-drawn carriages and wagons, and columns of mounted soldiers slowly moved forward. Riding in a carriage behind the Emperor were Bao-bao and his mother. They looked through the window at the familiar landscape and faces, feeling sad at parting from their home, and friends.

The chanting faded after the last wagon had gone by, the dust settled, and life in Lin Yu village returned to normal, harsh and isolated as ever. While the villagers drifted back to reality from the fairy-tale-like events that had taken place in the temple, the returning hunting party of the Emperor wound its way southward along the bumpy road. As the day advanced, they entered a forest. The late autumn sun shimmered through a canopy of tall weeping willows; here and there a few birds hopped around, eating insects from the mossy ground. Bao-bao sat by the window gazing at the passing scenes, changing yet changeless. His mother had dozed off. Suddenly he saw a monkey squatting on the branch of a tree. "Tartar!" he called. The monkey jumped onto the bare branch of another tree closer to the road and nodded at him; then, it was gone. A gentle breeze rolled across the canopy of the willow trees as Bao-bao stared at the empty spot where Tartar had been. In the midst of the soft rustle of the tree leaves, a voice echoed: *Your destiny is written in the stars; no one but you yourself can change it. The stars shine at night when all is dark; you too will rise and shine from a humble start.*

RAYMOND WONG is a retired engineer who lives in San Francisco where he is currently pursuing a master of arts in creative writing at San Francisco State University.

VERANDAH PORCHE

Snapshots: Summer 1952

Skates clamped to sensible shoes
with a silver key, we cruised
from our front stoop across blue
stone sidewalks. Between two sisters,
I flew by the neighbor's yard
where ripe cherries dropped
from the giant tree, slow motion
onto opened bedsheets; up the side
street past the brown Masonic Temple
where grown men pretended to be elks or moose,
into the corner market where we voted
for Beauty: the new Miss Rheingold.
We stuffed the ballot box with Xs:
kisses for the ladies we would someday
be; and rolled to the rippling chords
of Sonya Box's Studio of Tap, Ballet
and Torture; past Sweeny's where
beer and wheezing tenor bars from
"That's How I Spell Ireland"
blew us away toward Leda, the cop's
snobby daughter who twirled a baton
with her tongue out. We never looked
where poor Mr. Martinetti
hanged himself last Halloween.
"No treats! We have no treats!"
his ragged children cried.

Never glanced toward Our Lady
of Perpetual Strangeness where massive
Sisters could kidnap us, perhaps, under
wide black habits. No, we glided, hours
after, back to our own twin sycamores,
their trunks big around as a hug;
whose limbs held ground to sky
like mom and dad. Home to the maze
of barberry hedge, the kitchen where
Chef Boyardee and Betty Crocker wed.
When Good Humor bells dimmed down
First Street toward dark,
I counted fireflies and
black-and-blue marks, shin to knee.
Still sidewalks vibrated
pins and needles through my soles,
the day's whole Show-and-Tell.

VERANDAH PORCHE runs Lifelines, a poetry project with elders and others who need a writing partner, from her home in Guilford, Vermont. Her books include *The Body's Symmetry* and *Glancing Off*.

FORSTER FREEMAN

Laughter
in the Pews

DID YOU SEE THE CARTOON of the two White Anglo-Saxon
Protestants engaged in conversation? One exclaims to the other with
alarm, "Here comes God! Look busy!"

It embarrasses me to admit that this is a cartoon of me. I have
had a problem with playfulness. Have you? Well, I know not everyone does. But a lot of us did receive impressions early in our lives
about taking life very seriously if we hope to become godly. It seemed
that correct doctrine and hard work were far more essential to the
useful, godly life than participating in the extravagant, spontaneous,
creative love of the divine.

One of the first messages I remember receiving about religion
was called the "doctrine of uses." I carried the concept around that
to please God and mommy and daddy I had to strive hard to understand correct religious beliefs and to accomplish selfless deeds for
others.

It does not surprise me then that I was attracted to a career in
one of the "helping professions," pastoral ministry. I strove to care
for others as perfectly as I could, much of the time avoiding taking
care of my own needs for fear I might be selfish. When I did take days
off, I kept busy, and usually didn't do much that was playful with my
wife and children, nor did I cultivate intimate friendships. When I
treated myself to snacking on corn chips, I selected the broken ones
so the whole ones would be there for someone else.

Could it be that in choosing a profession for loving other people, I was unconsciously motivated by a hope that I could earn love
from others and God? Some say the biggest challenge in the spiritual life is not to give love but to receive love gracefully. Without re-

ceiving it, we have nothing to give. It became clear to me that I must have misread the teachings of mom and dad and our church, because my parents knew how to have fun and frequently cautioned me in my super-conscientious, overworked adulthood: "Forster, you're doing too much." I think my sister must have caught the same virus I did, because my parents often made the same plea to her. In my case, the problem has sometimes manifested itself as guilt if I take a couple of hours to read a book or as a mild feeling of depression on a day off when it seemed to me I hadn't accomplished enough. That's really carrying it too far. It's self-defeating, which is to say grace-canceling, influx-blocking. Surely our creator intended our lives to have a higher percentage of fun. Charles Haddon Spurgeon once said, "Some ministers would make good martyrs. They're so dry, they would burn well."

It's a wonder that partway through my career I was attracted, along with my wife Julia, to take a year away from parishes to be on the staff of a center in the redwoods of the Santa Cruz Mountains called Well-Springs Relax and Rebound Center. There, ironically enough, I, the ultimate perfectionist, helped facilitate the emerging of each participant's true self as rigidities melted away through use of music, movement, art, massage, journaling, and meditation. The Center was a good match for my needs at that time. It was just the right combination, just as years earlier I had intuited that Julia provided our relationship a healthy balance. It was this same Julia who, as my college girlfriend, drew me into the surprising discovery that I could occasionally leave the campus of my all-male school for a weekend of enjoyment with her and actually perform better in my studies the following week.

A few years ago, I became interested in the Enneagram, the ancient system for understanding personality types from Middle Eastern traditions. The perfectionist, symbolized by the ant, is number one in this system of nine basic types. My wife is an enspirited type seven, one given to pleasure, whose symbol is the butterfly.

Being a number-one "picture-straightener," my hard-working ant personality will attempt to carry several times its own weight, and if I'm not vigilant, I readily lapse into laboring unreasonably to make everything excel and into resentment when I or others fall

Leah Olivier.
Pen-and-ink, 1996.

Voss Finn.
Type Seven.
Pen-and-ink, 1996.

short. Even when I intend to be playing on the golf course or tennis court, for example, I might exert such a tense effort to make a powerful swing that I miss the ball. But now, I am enjoying the accuracy and ease of sports that comes with relaxation. As the Enneagram theory suggests, ones have much to teach us about what can be improved; in other words, their desire to work includes working on themselves.

It has interested me, also, to read in recent years some enlightened commentary on what Jesus meant about perfection. The most recent is an article by Richard Woods on the joys of imperfection. Woods says,

> The paradox of real perfection lies in that wholeness, and therefore, holiness, results not merely from accepting our limitations and imperfections, but thereby transcending them. And this, not by rooting them out by sheer force of will, even if that were possible, but by letting them go.[1]

My images of Jesus and the saints have gradually been undergoing major renovation. Some of my early teachers impressed on me the dour picture of Jesus as reflected in most paintings and films, as a sober man who lived in poverty and social ostracism, continually preoccupied with a tragic mission, "a man of sorrows and acquainted with grief." How extreme, unfair, and life-denying such a one-sided view can be when represented as a total description of Jesus! For those who accept Jesus as a model, it is essential to keep in mind the repeated accounts of his work as a carpenter, and his fondness for wedding banquets with dancing, luscious meals, and celebrative gatherings. On one occasion he even rescued a host by abundantly replenishing the exhausted wine supply. He was known for doing his partying with "sinners" rather than with the self-consciously pious. He accepted an emotional woman's sensuous foot massage administered with oil, tears, and her hair. He sent Peter on an errand to retrieve a coin from a fish's mouth and made up sometimes-amusing parables, like the one about waking up a neighbor late at night.

The call to faith-full lightening-up has been impressed on me so repeatedly that I now often awaken to recognize that it's not the enemy but the spirit of love and wisdom who encourages me to let go "till all our strivings cease." I think I've heard this spirit posing questions to me, such as the following:

- How much time have you taken this month for solitary contemplation that renews you and our relationship or for the hilarity with friends that you cherish?
- Is it your belief that your world is dependent on your working wearily as Mr. Nice Guy, as though you were the creator, redeemer, and sanctifier?

So now I frequently give reminders to myself in response:

- Give yourself permission to take time to read for enjoyment, play the piano and guitar, dance, to revel in the sound of the spring peepers—even when there's work to be completed.
- Feel the sensations in your body and heart and don't forget skinny-dipping and walking wonderingly in the hills.

My spiritual practices are coming to have their chuckling side, along with the rest of my life. The motivation for this change was heightened when I heard of a mother in a pew castigating her child: "Stop that playing around. God doesn't like people to laugh in church."

And so I am beginning to find the conceptual error when I sing the hymn, *Work for the Night is Coming,* and I find significant meaning in the minor sounds of "Come, labor on. Who dares stand idle on the harvest plain...."

Now I like to remember a description of a group of monks who every morning "went down to the river and bathed their hearts in laughter." And when I listen to Mozart, I not only recall his composing *A Musical Joke,* but also hear the silliness that occasionally pops up in his pieces.

My long quest to lighten up in my attempts to live usefully with the gifts I've been given is bearing fruit. I can discern the signs of the Spirit in my approaching tasks as I adopt a more carefree sense that God and I are partners in creativity.

One of my daughters has actually bestowed on me a Certificate of the Right to Play:

By this certificate know ye that

Forster Freeman

is a lifetime member in good standing in
The Society of Childlike Persons
and is hereby and forever entitled to
walk in the rain, jump in mud puddles, collect rainbows, smell
flowers, blow bubbles, stop along the way, build sandcastles,
watch the moon and stars come out, say hello to everyone, go
barefoot, go on adventures, sing in the shower, have a merry
heart, read children's books, act silly . . . and is encouraged
to always remember the motto of the society:
It's never too late to have a happy childhood.

As I was about to enter my seventieth year, I realized that God must be accomplishing in me the setting-free and the regeneration project that he loves to fashion in all he's created. I inwardly exclaim, "I hear you, Lord. Thank you for your love that uses unexpected tongues and circumstances to take care of my need to see that you and I are slowly continuing our progress together." Perhaps I should teach our grandchildren a version of the doctrine of uses I call "playful uses." And I can tell them that even ants can have fun. Could it be that is what the Creator was doing during those first six days?

Leah Olivier.
Pen-and-ink, 1996.

FORSTER FREEMAN is a partly-retired ordained minister, teacher, and spiritual director with dual standing in the Presbyterian Church (USA) and the United Church of Christ.

Note

1. The joys of imperfection. *Presence: An International Journal of Spiritual Direction,*
   2 (1)(January, 1996):61.

RICHARD BALLON

Skater

Your blade winks,
raising pools upon the ice,
like a star cutting a cloud
for a momentary view.
It lures me.
Knowing should I choose
to walk on water
and our hands brush
through chance
I would fall

Though I want
I want to say:
It is the beauty of your face
not the sharpness of your blade
that forms the pools to hold you near.

Don't ask my name, just kiss me.

But I would be a leaf chasing the wind
that drives it.
The tattooed ice
that urges the skater on.

RICHARD BALLON lives, works, and dreams in New England. He is currently writing and directing a six-part mini-series, for his community local access television station.

Veyanie

BROWN FIELDS. One bare tree on the horizon. A solitary figure along the road, heavy boots crumbling the edges of frozen ruts. He reaches into a pocket of his shabby coat, pulls out a small tin flute, and begins to play as he walks.

The notes trill out in a cascade of crystal. There is an answering bird song from a copse, hesitant, hopeful. The little breezes in the dale suddenly seem warmer and hurry after him through the brown tufts of grass.

He passes several farmsteads. The barns look snug, and the farmhouses have new coats of white paint. Children chase each other through the neat farmyards, shrieking happily.

Higher up, in the big hills, he comes upon a small hard-scrabble farm seemingly glued to the hillside. Patches of dirty snow lie in the shadows. A woman stands on the sagging porch, yelling at two children in the yard. "Din't I say git your chores done? Do I have to do everything myself?"

She shakes a frying pan at them as she shouts and finally throws it down in frustration. It lands with a thud on the frozen ground. The small boy flinches, but the young girl stands defiant.

"Git in that barn an' git to work right now!"

The boy scurries off, but the girl stands her ground and holds the woman's eyes for a moment, then slowly turns and follows her brother to the barn.

The woman watches them go, hands on her hips, easing her back. Wisps of dishwater-colored hair hang down around her face. She pushes them back with a damp hand. Sighs. Then she looks up and catches sight of the man coming down the hill.

"Ain't got no food for no beggars," she says when he's close enough.

"Please Missus, I am looking for work. My back is strong."

"Cain't afford no help. There's plenty of places back along the road that can pay you for your strong back."

"Yes, I saw them." The man stands before her, not smiling, but his eyes are warm like brown nuts roasting. "I will work for my supper and a warm place to sleep."

She frowns, studying him. The hair curling from beneath his cap is grizzled, but his face is so smooth and full of life that his age can't be guessed.

"Not from around here?"

"No, I am traveling."

"Where to?"

"Just traveling. To see things."

"What things?"

"I never know what they may be until I see them."

"Well, you look strong enough. Guess you could earn your supper right enough. I do need help. Start with the wood. We're real low."

"I will chop you enough wood to build a house!" he says, walking over to the woodpile. He flashes a big-toothed grin at the woman and raises the ax over his head in a salute.

Thomas Hart Benton.
Woodchopper.
Tempera on masonite,
$17^7/8 \times 14^1/8$ inches,
1936. Tucson: The
University of Arizona
Museum of Art. Gift of
Mrs. Fred Greiner
(79.1.1).

"Just chop enough to build me a fire!" she retorts, and disappears into the house.

The farmhouse is so small the downstairs is one room. In this room where there is usually no bed lies a tall thin man in a narrow bed. He looks up without interest as the woman enters.

"I done hired us a man to help out, Frank. He says he'll work for food and a place to sleep. I reckon we still got enough potatoes to feed one more, even if he is a big'un. He's chopping wood right now."

Frank turns his head and looks out the window.

"It ain't your fault, Frank. You didn't fall off the barn roof on purpose, and you didn't bring this god-awful winter on us."

"I know, Esther," but he keeps staring out the window. She stands watching him a minute then busies herself by the stove.

The man is still chopping when the little boy comes across the yard.

"Hey, Mister! That's some pile of wood you done chopped! There weren't no wood here at all awhile ago."

The man thumps himself on the chest. "I am very strong!—But I am lonely. Please, you can keep me company? Or are there more chores for you?"

"I'm done now."

"Good! then you will talk to me. Tell me about your travels on the seven seas!" The man looks expectant.

"I ain't even seen the sea!"

"Oh? Everyone should see the sea, you know. But for now, let us sing a song instead. A lumberjack song is a good song to sing while chopping wood, yes?"

"I guess so, but I don't know no lumberjack song. My ma says I can't carry a tune if it had a handle on it."

"Yes? Well, everyone can't do everything. You like music though? Maybe I show you how you can sing." And he pulls the little flute out of his pocket.

"That's pretty!" says the boy, admiring its glint in a stray shaft of sunlight.

"It will be even prettier in a moment, when you play it."

"I can't play no flute."

"Certainly you can! See how easy," and the man puts the flute to his lips. A lively jig bounces through the farmyard. "You try. See, you hold it like this, and put your fingers so. Then you lift your fingers for each note. Try it."

The boy gives a tentative toot. Then he tries a few notes and finally whistles a shaky scale.

"Good! You practice while I chop. You can entertain me in a fine concert hall! Try to play a song you know. Something simple. *Three Blind Mice?*"

"I know that!" At first the effort sounds more like a cock fight, but the man grins his big grin and keeps chopping. Soon *Three Blind Mice* can be heard quavering through the cold air.

The woman comes across the farmyard.

"Frankie, where'd you get that?"

"He lent it to me," says Frankie, pointing at the man among the huge piles of wood. "He's teaching me to play! I done all my chores."

"Don't bother him, Frankie, he's got his own chores to do."

"He is not bothering me, but keeping a lonely traveler company. You can see I have not been lazy."

"You sure got wood choppin' down to an art," she concedes.

"And listen to what I can play, Ma!" Frankie interrupts, and puts the flute to his lips.

"Well, that's a tune, all right. I reckon it won't harm you none. I'm going to milk the cows. Where's Dodie?"

"I don't know. She went into the woods."

The woman sighs deeply, "You'll have to help me with the milkin' then."

"Please Missus," the man says, "I am very good with cows. I will milk. You go and rest. Let me go to the cows."

"Well, I don't have no time for resting, but maybe I can get supper on the table a bit earlier. You go and milk, then."

"Yes Missus!" He says it as if he has won a prize. "You keep practicing, Mister Frankie, and after supper you will play us a concert!"

When the supper bell rings, the man comes from the barn to find Frankie still tootling away on the woodpile.

"Where can I wash, please?"

"What for? You don't look that dirty to me," says Frankie, peering through his fringe of grimy hair.

"Don't you wash for supper? It is a very good habit, you know. All the best kings and princes do it."

"They do? Are you sure?" asks Frankie suspiciously.

"Oh yes, absolutely sure. All the best queens and princesses, too," he adds. Dodie has just come into the farmyard from the woods.

"Well, all right, I guess so." Frankie starts across the yard to a pump that had been hidden by a half-fallen shed.

"You too, Miss?" the man says gently to Dodie. She looks off to the side for a moment before she realizes he's addressing her.

"Yes, of course!" she blurts out. "Of course I wash for supper!" She looks as if water hasn't touched her young skin for many days. Dodie follows Frankie, and the man walks behind.

After washing, they all troop onto the porch and into the house. The table is covered with a clean checkered cloth, and the oil lamp set in the middle has a freshly polished chimney.

"The table looks nice, Ma!" says Dodie, surprised.

"I had a few extra minutes."

Esther doesn't look at the man. Frank slowly gets up from where he's sitting on the edge of the bed and lowers himself gingerly into his chair. Frankie bounces into the chair beside him.

Esther wraps a rag around the handle of the pot steaming on the stove and carries it to the table where she puts it down with a thump. She begins ladling the contents into tin plates.

"It smells wonderful!" says the man, eyes bright with expectation.

"Ain't nothing but plain potato stew. Lucky to have a bit of bacon left to flavor it," says Esther.

"Hunger makes the best sauce, my grandmother always said, so I am sure it is the most delicious stew I have ever eaten!" says the man, flashing his big-toothed smile.

They pass around the plates, break apart a loaf of hard bread, and Esther sits down. After thorough attention is given to the thin stew, Frank says, "Mister, I guess we don't even know your right name."

"It is Veyanie," says the man.

"That's a funny name. What's it mean? "

"Drift."

"Drift! That's good then, cause you're a drifter, right!" says Frank, pleased at making a joke.

"Yes!" laughs Veyanie, "but drift, you know, it also means what the wind does, you cannot see it, but it is strong; it drifts the sand and the snow."

After supper they sit around the wood stove. "It's nice and warm tonight!" Dodie says happily. Esther is staring dreamily at the flickering oil lamp.

"Now we have some music, I think!" says Veyanie. "Frankie is going to play music for us!" Frankie jumps up and pulls out the flute.

"Listen everybody! Listen what I can do!" and he plays *Three Blind Mice* with such enthusiasm, and only one wrong note, that his audience claps in surprise and delight.

"Very good!" says Veyanie. "Now if I may borrow back my instrument, I will continue the concert."

The room fills with a rollicking jig, which soon gets Dodie off her feet to bound around the room with Frankie. The children whirl around as Veyanie plays and thumps his heavy boots in time. Then the children grasp Esther's hands and pull her into their dance. They laugh over her protests and whirl her around until she falls breathless into her chair.

"Now, that's enough of that foolishness for me, understand!" she says, settling firmly back into the chair. But her cheeks are flushed, and her eyes are bright.

Frank pats her on the arm. "You look right pretty tonight, Esther."

"Everyone's so silly tonight!" but she looks pleased, and this time the flush is not from the dance.

The next morning Veyanie tells them he is moving on. "Here, Frankie," he says, pulling the flute from a pocket. "You may keep this. You must promise to practice so everyone can dance to your music, yes?"

"Thanks! Thanks a lot! I'll practice, I promise."

They watch the man walk away up the road. After he's over the hill and they can see him no longer, he reaches into his bundle and pulls out another flute from the dozen or so that lay wrapped in old newspaper in the bottom of his bundle.

The notes trill out in a cascade of crystal, and the answering bird song comes from all around him. The little breezes spread their warmth in an arc that marks his passing.

ANGELA WERNER, who lives in Springtown, Pennsylvania, notes that *veyanie* is a Russian word, meaning "to drift." Chiefly through promulgation by the writer and critic Apollyon Grigoryev, the word has figuratively come to mean "ephemeral, but of palpable influence." It was reading this in Grigoryev's autobiography that inspired her to write a story about a character that embodied this meaning.

ELSA BETHANIS

The Frog Prince

Deep under mud I waited.
When the princesses came, I flopped behind,
careful to avoid their spiked heels.

With hormone pills and thirty-six operations,
the warts have shrunk.

Tall now, handsome enough,
with a good golf swing,
I squat on the back barstool,
watching the dancers flit under lights.

You've seen me, with flies
stuffed in my pockets,
scars on my belly and hands.
You know who I am.
I wait for your kiss,
your head against my damp white chest,
your arms around my sagging waist.

ELSA BETHANIS received a master of fine arts degree from the University of Massachusetts at Amherst. Her work has appeared or is forthcoming in several literary magazines, including *Icon, Negative Capability,* and *The Cape Rock.*

IRVING MACE

In Search of the Ultimate Rush

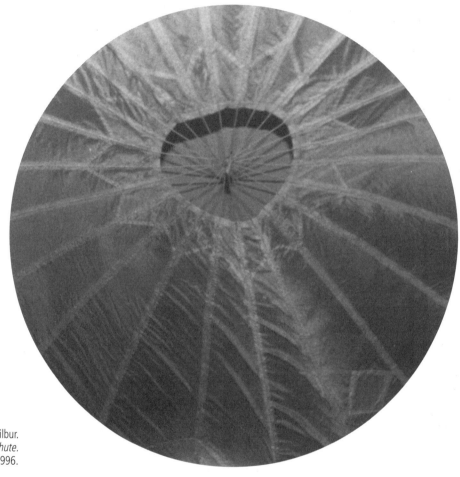

Barbara Wilbur.
Parachute.
Photograph, 1996.

IT WAS NEVER ENOUGH just to be in step. Whatever the majority did, I did something different. If the people went left, I went right. Black was white, and white was boring. I, for some unknown reason, enjoyed risking a jump into gray areas where few others would dare tread, much less jump. If society said that a certain thing was wrong or too dangerous, I would decide to prove society wrong. Needless to say, such an attitude of rebelliousness, especially in a young and naive mind, can end up taking its toll. In my case, I became a hard-core junkie. Even though I have been in recovery for eleven years, my search for the ultimate rush has continued.

I WAS SHOOTING ALONG THE ROAD in Zephryhills, Florida, on my Harley, when suddenly, up in the sky, a bunch of colorful forms appeared before my eyes like balloons at a birthday party. I happened to be riding by an internationally known skydiving school. I saw a sign: Skydive City—Tandem Jumping—Spectators Welcome. I decided to pull in. Because it was a weekday, the place was relatively calm compared to weekends when it is crowded with skydivers from all over the world.

It didn't take long before I was introduced to TK, manager of Skydive City. Although there are other tandem-qualified skydivers at Skydive City, TK agreed to take me up personally. The following morning, as agreed, my butterflies and I went back to Skydive City. The entire process was easier than expected, which is why tandem jumping has become so popular. According to TK, were it not for the success of tandem jumping, there would be only half as many solo skydivers as there are now. Jumping tandem under one parachute provides the exact same experience as jumping solo.

After signing a few liability forms and watching a video, TK took me through every step of the skydive. Soon I was being squeezed into a Twin Otter airplane, flying up to 13,500 feet, where I would jump along with a dozen experts who would be exiting the plane just before me. Our flight would be videotaped by May Ahlberg, a professional "camera flyer" from Sweden, who has logged in as many hours in the sky as some motorcyclists have on their scooters. May would also take some still shots from a helmet camera triggered by biting down on a small device inside the mouth.

Because my butterflies were flying long before me, they had me asking TK if we were up to 13,500 feet yet. The ground had become a cloudy blur. Holding his altimeter in front of me, I could see that we had another 10,000 feet to go. What have I gotten myself into this time? I thought as the plane continued to shudder on up. As we passed through the stratus but not my fear, my butterflies had babies. At 13,500 feet everything happened fast but not before the experts took quick glances back at me. Next to the jump itself, I just knew that they were all enjoying what the butterflies had obviously done to my face. In seconds they were out the door. I was now on my knees, at once leaning outside the door and saying a quick prayer, all the while strapped tightly in my harness to TK. May was literally hanging outside the door, waiting for us to exit. I gave the camera a phony smile and jumped. ARCH! ARCH! ARCH! I repeated to myself.

After tumbling a bit, TK had us facing back down toward mother earth at over 120 mph. The roaring free fall through cumulus clouds and blue sky lasted a full minute. Out of nowhere as if she were some angel floating in front of me, May appeared, capturing it all on film. Once the chute opened, the rest of the ride down took another five or six minutes. We landed safely and comfortably even though the two of us totaled well over 400 pounds. And there again was May with her camera, having landed about two minutes earlier.

Why do skydivers jump from planes? Not because we're crazy, but because the door is open, and this is our way to play.

BEING AN OBSESSIVE–COMPULSIVE RECOVERING JUNKIE, two days after making the tandem jump I went back to Skydive City. Knowing that I would be taught by some of the top skydivers in the world, I signed up for the Accelerated Free Fall course, which consists of learning seven basic levels of skydiving.

During the three days it took to pass my first five levels, the fear factor was kept at a minimum. For some unexplainable reason, however, just before and during my Level-6 skydive, I found myself in a barely controllable state of panic. But since the entire sport of skydiving is centered around various degrees of an adrenaline rush, it didn't seem to matter. If skydiving didn't bring skydivers to the verge of an adrenaline overdose, there probably wouldn't be any skydivers; adrenaline is what these types of extreme sports are all about. No adrenaline, no sport, no play, it's that simple. In any case, during my Level-6, which was actually my twelfth skydive, I couldn't find the handle to open my chute. While falling to earth like a fat rock, my hand, as if placed there by the wind, finally found and pulled the handle, and the parachute opened. Needless to say, I was given a new perspective on my mortality.

Later that evening I asked my Higher Power to give me a sign as to whether or not I should continue skydiving. That night I had a skydiving nightmare in which my main parachute failed to open. When I tried to pull the handle on my reserve, nothing happened. I just kept falling and falling to earth, never hitting the ground until I woke up in a cold sweat. Could this have been the sign that I had asked for? If it was, it wasn't clear enough, and I didn't take heed.

The following morning I was back at Skydive City, still willing to take my Level-6—Jump 13—over again. But my level of adrenaline, rather than waiting for me to be at the open door of an airplane at 13,500 feet, was now with me on the ground. I could only imagine what it would be like when I was actually at the door waiting to jump. But if I wanted to be a skydiver, I knew that I would have to control my fear, otherwise my fear would control me, perhaps even on the ground. If I let that happen, I might just end up selling my Harley and locking myself in a sterilized room for the rest of my boring life.

Ken, May's husband, would be jumping with me and evaluating my performance. Even though he was a competent, thoroughly trained, experienced skydiver, Ken had never been on a Level-6 skydive before as a Jump Master. This increased my apprehension even more, as did the fact that I had packed my own parachute for the very first time—under supervision. During one minute, or approximately 9,000 feet of free fall time, I was expected to do two backloops, locate the airport and track toward the airport.

After completing the above maneuvers to the best of my ability, I pulled the handle of my main parachute. Partly because I was in the wrong position at the time and partly because these things just happen, if only on the rarest of occasions, my main canopy malfunctioned, staying locked in its container. I only saw the little white drogue chute fluttering above my head like an ominous halo. At about 2,500 feet, the bare minimum allowed for the deployment of my reserve canopy, Ken suddenly appeared before me, just as May had done while filming my tandem jump, signaling me to cut away and pull my reserve, which is what I was about to do anyway. Believe it or not, I was able to remain relatively calm the entire time, if only because I had been trained for such an emergency beforehand.

After cutting away my main canopy, I pulled the reserve and watched it suddenly appear above my head, replacing the useless drogue chute. It was as if a silken guardian had come to save me, which of course it was, and did. I had been given yet another last chance. After looking at my altimeter, I saw that I was now only 1,000 feet above the ground. I then proceeded to steer my parachute safely to an open field, complete with cows and plenty of mother earth, which I kissed in gratitude and understanding of a clear message that was finally received.

IRVING MACE, who lives in Massachusetts, is a freelance travel and outdoors writer. He reviews Florida campgrounds for a publishing company and gives seminars on the therapeutic values of family camping.

ALICE B. SKINNER

Re-creating the Mind

Matteo Radoslovich.
Pumpkin Figure Head.
Painted wood, metal,
pumpkin, 11×26 inches,
twentieth century.
New York: Museum of
American Folk Art. Gift
of Dorothy and Leo
Rabkin (1983.17.18).

AT PLAY, WE LEAP AWAY FROM THE MUNDANE, the routine. We notice the unexpected and take a chance on it . . .

Someone dancing inside us
learned only a few steps:
the "Do Your Work" in 4/4 time,
the "What-Do-You-Expect" waltz.
He hasn't noticed yet the woman
standing away from the lamp,
the one with black eyes

who knows the rhumba,
and strange steps in jumpy rhythms
from the mountains in Bulgaria.
If they dance together,
something unexpected will happen.
If they don't, the next world
will be a lot like this one.[1]

We track nuances and discover implications.

Two boys uncoached are tossing a poem together,
overhand, underhand, backhand, sleight of hand, every hand,
Teasing with attitudes, latitudes, interludes, altitudes,
High, make him fly off the ground for it, low, make him stoop,
Make him scoop it up, make him as-almost-as-possible miss it,
Fast, let him sting from it, now, now fool him slowly,
Anything, everything tricky, risky, nonchalant,
Anything under the sun to outwit the prosy,
Over the tree and the long sweet cadence down,
Over his head, make him scramble to pick up the meaning,
And now, like a posy, a pretty one plump in his hands.[2]

Wassily Kandinsky.
Jocular Sounds. Oil on
cardboard, 48.9×34.9
cm., 1929. Cambridge:
The Harvard University
Art Museums. From the
Busch–Reisinger
Museum in memory
of Eda K. Loeb and
Association Fund
(BR56.54).

[1] Bill Holm. "Advice." In Robert Bly, James Hillman, and Michael Meade, eds.
The Rag and Bone Shop of the Heart. New York: Harper Perennial, 1993. p.14.
[2] Robert Francis. "Catch." Ibid. p. 186.

*Alice B.
Skinner*

Boardman Robinson.
Judson Stoddard.
Gouache on masonite,
10¾ × 14½ inches,
ca. 1944. Tucson: The
University of Arizona
Museum of Art. Gift of
C. Leonard (x45.9.38).

Play enchants, stirring the imagination, moving us to new understandings.

> My eyes already touch the sunny hill,
> going far ahead of the road I have begun.
> So we are grasped by what we cannot grasp;
> it has its inner light, even from a distance
>
> and changes us, even if we do not reach it,
> into something else, which, hardly sensing it,
> > we already are . . .[3]

[3] Rainer Maria Rilke. "A Walk." In Robert Bly, trans. *Selected Poems of Rainer Maria Rilke.* New York: Harper & Row, 1981. p. 177.

Play invites zest, gaiety, a "quest for the superfluous." [4]

    Man's chief difference from the brutes lies
in the exuberant excess of his subjective
propensities—his pre-eminence over them
simply and solely in the number and in the
fantastic and unnecessary character of his
wants, physical, moral, aesthetic, and
intellectual . . . Prune down his extravagance,
sober him, and you undo him. [4]

Andrew Wyeth.
Winter Carnival.
Drybrush, $23^7/8 \times 22\frac{1}{4}$
inches, 1985.
Private collection.

---

[4] William James. "On Extravagant Desires." In Robert Bly, James Hillman, and Michael
Meade, eds. *The Rag and Bone Shop of the Heart*. New York: Harper Perennial, 1993.

Play transforms the ordinary with extravagance.

I fear chiefly lest my expression may not be
extra vagant enough, may not wander far enough
beyond the narrow limits of my daily experience,
so as to be adequate to the truth of which I
have been convinced. *Extra vagance!* It depends
on how you are yarded . . .[5]

Joan Miró.
La Naissance du Jour.
Gouache,ink
and watercolor on paper
43¹/₄×31¹/₈ inches,
1942. Tucson: The
University of Arizona
Museum of Art. Gift of
Edward J. Gallagher Jr.
(56.6.1)

**Diversions, "various enjoyments and pleasures of bodily senses
recreate the mind,"[6] but our motivations determine how we are
"yarded."**

Diversions will vary according to the affections within each
mind. Diversions are one thing if the affection of charity is
present, another if there is only an affection for honor there,
another if it is an affection only for gain, another if we perform our duties only for the sake of self-maintenance, another
if only for prestige or if only for profits to make us rich or to
let us live in pleasure, and so on . . . [7]

---

[5] Henry David Thoreau. "On Being Extravagant." In Robert Bly, James Hillman,
and Michael Meade, eds. *The Rag and Bone Shop of the Heart.* New York: Harper
Perennial, 1993. p. 163.

[6] Emanuel Swedenborg. *Charity: The Practice of Neighborliness.* West Chester,
Pennsylvania: Swedenborg Foundation, 1995. Paragraph no. 189.

[7] Ibid. Paragraph no. 191–192.

Play connects our whole being with the universe.

> Between the conscious and the unconscious, the
>   mind has put up a swing:
> All earth creatures, even the supernovas, sway
>   between these two trees,
> and it never winds down.
>
> Angels, animals, humans, insects by the million,
>   also the wheeling sun and moon;
> ages go by, and it goes on.
> Everything is swinging: heaven, earth, water, fire ...[8]

Mark Tobey. *Toward the Light [Dem Licht Entgegen].* Oil on canvas, $16^{1}/8 \times 20^{1}/16$ inches, ca. 1930. Tucson: The University of Arizona Museum of Art. Museum Funds provided by the Edward J. Gallagher Jr. Memorial Fund (81.11.1).

[8] Kabir. "Between the conscious and the unconscious." In Stephen Mitchell, ed. *The Enlightened Heart: An Anthology of Sacred Poetry.* New York: Harper & Row, 1989. p. 70.

And reaches beyond.
He who binds to himself a joy
Does the winged life destroy.
But he who kisses the joy as it flies
Lives in eternity's sun rise.[9]

William Blake. *Albion Rose*. Intaglio etching / engraving, ca. 1793. San Marino, California: The Henry E. Huntington Library and Art Gallery (HEH 000.124).

ALICE B. SKINNER, who is art editor for the Chrysalis Reader, holds a master's degree in social work from the University of Minnesota and a doctorate degree in psychology from Harvard University.

[9] William Blake. "Eternity." In Alicia Ostriker, ed. *The Complete Poems*. ed. Harmondsworth, Middlesex, England: Penguin Books, 1977, reprinted 1985. p. 153.

 Unwritten Rules

**LISTEN! YOU CAN'T JUST PLAY AT PLAYING!
DO IT RIGHT! LEARN THE RULES!**

The first rule is: FORGET THE RULES.

The second rule is: IF YOU DON'T KNOW HOW TO PLAY,
PLAY BY THE RULES. When all else fails,
read the instructions.

*Like all good advice, these rules need
interpretation. Forgetting the rules
is effective only when you are playing
too hard to remember them. When the
"One Great Scorer" counts how you played
the game, high marks come from playing
with wholehearted, full-bore participation.*

*Those who have given their wholehearted,
full-bore participation to the cultural ideal
of doing—often with "thin lips and troubled gut"
(as Forster Freeman in Part I so aptly says)—
need to read the rules of play again.*

KATY LENZ

How to Play without a Friend

I'M FIFTEEN NOW, but I can remember how it felt when I was ten, and I can tell you that even by yourself you can play games that aren't boring. You never start losing these games, so you never have to quit.

If it's a good day outside, you can play a really great game I invented. Don't tell your sister about it because she'll laugh at you. Don't tell your mom either, because she'll tell all her friends, and they'll all laugh about it. Remember mom's rule: No leaving the yard or woods. Even if your yard is boring, there's plenty of good stuff in it for this game.

You have to pick a name. Mine is Princess Lily. Then you have to turn your yard into a kingdom. It sounds hard, but it's not. I'll tell you about my kingdom.

First of all, our house is the castle. From now on call it the castle, or the game is wrecked. Next to the castle is the Royal Servant's House, which has yellow flowers growing all over it. Inside is the Wise Old Magician, who likes to tell me secrets. He usually disguises himself as a dog, but, if you call him a dog name, it'll make him angry. If your sister comes over and asks you why you're sitting in the bush talking to the dog, ignore her.

Next, take a stroll of the Royal Gardens. Tell your servant that the beans are growing excellently. Do not walk on a bean plant or the servant will magically turn back into your angry mother.

Over there is the Summer Palace, which I own. You better find a palace too, because sometimes, if you go in the castle, the evil witch

Opposite:
Maxine Albro. *Skipping.*
Oil on canvas,
21½×25¼ inches,
ca. 1940. Tucson: The
University of Arizona
Museum of Art.
Gift of C. Leonard
Pfeiffer (x45.8.1).

will make you her slave and make you wash dishes. If the hay is old and dirty, that's only because the royal horses live there. Climb up in the loft of the Summer Palace. Look down over your kingdom. Make a speech.

Next, you can visit the village and talk to the common people. Watch out for your mom again because she'll mess it up by telling you not to walk in the strawberry patch. (It's actually best to play this game if everyone else is in the castle.)

Go pick some blueberries in the Royal Orchards. If you want, you can go into the woods to see some more of the kingdom, but the people there are rough and scratchy. The main reason to go there is to visit the Princess Lily River. Don't call it a creek.

There are many things to visit on Princess Lily River, like Rock Island, the first stop from the path. This is a good place to dip your feet in, but watch out for the terrible current which could suck you in. Watch the waterfall. Don't bring boys down to the river because they'll block up the waterfall with dirt and try to catch fish. To the south of Rock Island is Fern House and Cave Slide and also the Secret Meadow. To the north is Great Tree Overlook, the Cliffs of Moss, and the Log Bridge.

On some days, if it's starting to rain, you have to find a good game for indoors. You're lucky I know one. It's called Countryhouse People. First you need a lot of little dolls called Countryhouse People. When your mom gets you some, they'll have FISHER-PRICE on the label, but that's not the real name, and it's dumb anyhow. You can play this game with your sister, but it's best not to because she makes up idiot stories and pretends to swallow the people. Then, when mom comes in the room, she says she didn't put them in her mouth, and mom won't even check to see that the person is all wet.

The only way to play this game is to have tons of Countryhouse People and give them all names. It's not hard to name them, just name them after how they look, and you'll never forget the name. The one with a top hat is Mr. Millionaire, the one with a western hat is Cowboy Steve, and the one with an apron on is Joe the shopkeeper. Sometimes they just don't look like anything, so name them Susan or Bob or Mike or Lisa or Brandon or Moe or Kelly.

Decide which people go in which families and build them all houses from blocks. You'll just have to pretend there's a roof because if you build one, you can't see into the house, and that's no good. Mr. Millionaire gets the big plastic house since it's the best. He's going to need it though because he has a lot of children, like Daisy and Lisa and Violet and Kelly and Oliver and Baby Jeffrey. If it's a holiday, or if you feel like it, you can build a big house for all of them to stay in. Put a ballroom in it and a living room and whatever else you want.

Something else that's fun is to build a room and put all the best furniture and things in it and make it into a clubhouse. Then build an obstacle course, and make the people go through it to get to the clubhouse. Or you can build a maze out of dominoes instead of the obstacle course.

If you decide to make every family have their own house, you can make a village. Streets should just be bare floor, and sidewalks should be dominoes. You have to have a restaurant and an office, but, if you want to make up something else, you can. That's why it's best to have blocks, so you can make something new every time. Set up your village or big hotel or maze or whatever and leave it there. Cry if mom tells you that you have to take it down. If you make a really good one, maybe she'll let you keep it up. Make your people have adventures. Make your favorite one the hero every time. Your favorite Countryhouse person should look like you.

This game will usually make you tired, so find your favorite doll and get in your bed. If you can't go to sleep right away, think of all the games you'll play tomorrow and all the stuff you'll do. Don't worry about nightmares because favorite dolls have magical monster-protection. Think up new stories for your Countryhouse People. Think that the dogwood tree in the yard would be a good lookout tower for the approach of enemies to your kingdom. Fall asleep . . .

KATY LENZ is a junior at Buckingham County High School in Virginia, but she vividly remembers the games she played when she was younger. She still owns fifty-three "Countryhouse" people, but her lookout tower has been cut down.

Sunny Lenz and
Arianna Arbo-Yay.
Pencil, 1996.

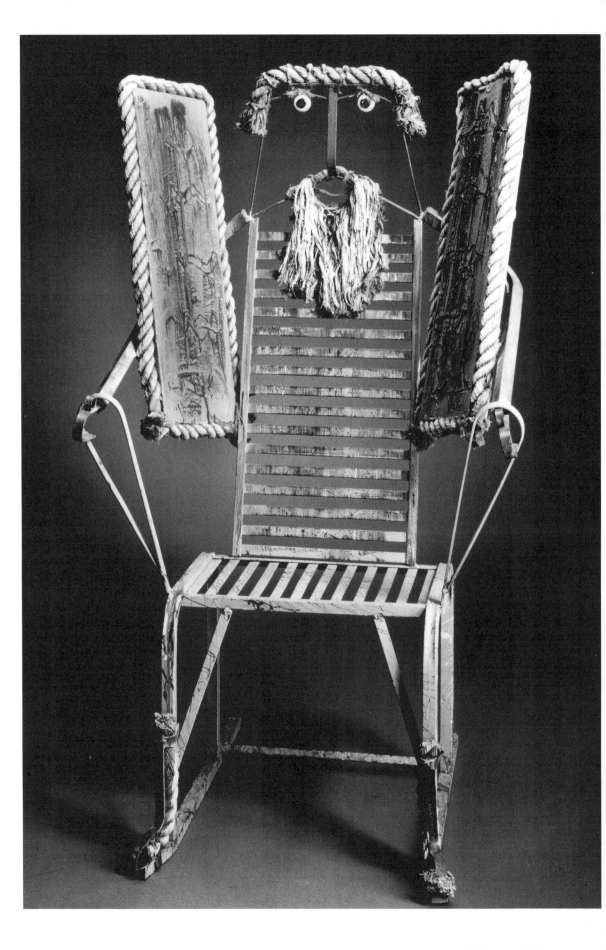

J. THEODORE KLEIN
AND KATHERINE STANNARD

Be-attitudes of Play

SPUNKY, A CAT, BATS AT A TWIST OF PAPER ON A STRING. She needs no one to teach her to play. The paper becomes an object of affection or prey, eliciting a pat or a bite. It moves in unexpected ways, obliging Spunky to adapt her movements to continue the play. She is learning body movements, trajectories, reactions—all needed to become a successful adult cat. It appears that play is school for animals, and it is school for human beings as well.

Play is our universal language. In play we find discovery, mystery, and pleasure for all participants. Play touches us personally, professionally, and artistically. As we experiment with play, we grow and develop and create something new. We need play to evolve into healthy, happy, and productive adults.

In parallel play, often seen in preschool children, play may take place through association without interaction. Susie and Jimmy play side-by-side, on two different scenarios. For Jimmy, the sandbox provides material for a house in which his little dinosaurs can dwell. For Susie, it is a construction site for her trucks. All may go well until Susie's road needs to go through the middle of Jimmy's house. Then we have frustration and battle, or perhaps adaptation into cooperation. The road can follow a different path; houses sometimes can be moved. Here the be-attitude is be-beside, be-with, companionship, and even cooperation.

When Susie and Jimmy go to school, they will seek out other children for a "nine-guys-on-a-side" baseball game and other rule-governed play. Initially, rules tend to be sacrosanct, and eight guys to

Opposite:
Richard Dial. *Comfort of Moses.* Steel, wood, hemp, and enamel paint, 33x57×32½ inches, 1988. New York: Museum of American Folk Art. Museum of American Folk Art purchase made possible with grants from the National Endowment for the Arts and the Metropolitan Life Foundation (1990.3.5).

a side won't work. Later, rules can be changed. Play is Susie's way of learning the rules of her world.

In the best of all worlds, play continues into adulthood. Our friend Nancy teaches adult classes in quilt-making, setting problems of size, shape, design, and color, requiring fine needle skills and all amidst in social interaction that produces a piece of work. Not much different from colonial quilting bees; our ancestors knew something about cooperative work and play.

Consider Bill and Joan on an autumn day. Leaves change from green to flame, blazing on the hillsides, astonishing on the streets. Tightly wrapped in wooly sweaters, they stroll along a narrow wooded lane, neither speaking, frost forming in their hearts—a contrast with their bright surroundings. An impudent gust of wind sets sail an armada of wine oak leaves that makes landfall in their sweaters. Both begin to pick away at the clinging vegetation, but suddenly Joan picks up an armful of leaves from the pathway and throws them at Bill, who is immediately feathered with more leaves. What did she think she was doing? Bill, caught off guard, retaliates with his own leafy ammunition. Immersed in autumn color, smell, and texture, both rocket into childhood and amaze themselves by laughing. The feint becomes a contest: greater bundles of leaves, bodies turning and bending, a skid into the leaves. Joan, losing her balance, lunges toward Bill, who grabs her leafy arm and sets her upright. The saving grasp turns into a hug, and both hold each other, laughing.

Cheerfully dusting each other off and resuming their walk, they both stop, transfixed. Four school-age children busy themselves on a leafy carpeted lawn. Each child wields a small rake, industriously working leafy raw material into neat rows that cross each other at intervals. Occasionally a shout "We need a door here to get out," or, "Let's make two rooms out of this one," as the children develop their patterns. "A leaf house!" cries Joan. "How many of those I made, and how many blew away!" "Good little workers," observes Bill. "I've got to rake for real when we get home." "Glad to help you, sir," Joan smiles.

Adults and children encountered leaves in varied settings, and all used leaves for play. For the two adults, play began almost by accident, transforming a tense relationship into a burst of affection. The leaf-war began spontaneously and led to an unexpected reconciliation, unforeseen consequences. For the children, patterns and rules developed among them as their play progressed, leading to further cooperative activity within the walls of their leaf house. In both events, a be-attitude allowed the participants to create something new from simple materials. Freedom and imagination served as catalysts for pleasure and discovery.

And, in the case of Joan and Bill, play activities suggested a move toward yard work but with cooperation between them and the promise of latent play to blossom into further pleasure. Later, no doubt, the children will rake as work, earning allowances, helping the family, and even grumbling at the leaves. What makes these differences? Probably, in good part, the be-attitude of the players: be free, be rule-governed, be productive—the range from free play to structured play to work itself.

The line between work and play is tissue-thin. At a writers conference, for example, Bob described getting out of bed at 3 AM when the right word suddenly revealed itself. Writing supersedes sleeping, and even eating. When words flow, Bob enters a state of joy, transcendence. His work, from which he makes his living, is play. And sometimes pretty solitary.

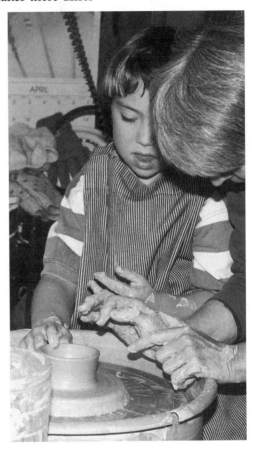

Last week we sat with a half dozen adults whose task involved evaluation of others' work. A serious business. But as work proceeded, words flowed more freely. Personal anecdotes of writer's block and writer's victories were shared, outrageous puns and jokes punctuated conversation, and work became playful while retaining its goal-directed nature. A be-attitude of doing a good piece of work with a light spirit, be-joyful.

Understanding play's value for children's learning and development, we must ensure that children have many play opportunities, for their health and for ours. Children who have met joy in play are ready to give joy to others. Play is an oasis in the adult world of obligation. The ultimate be-attitude is playful thought, playful action, and playful community.

The line between play and work is thin.

J. THEODORE KLEIN is a professor of theology and philosophy at the Swedenborg School of Religion in Newton, Massachusetts. He is the father of three children ranging in age from teen to young adult. KATHERINE STANNARD taught undergraduates about children's play as a professor of psychology at Framingham State College in Massachusetts. She is the mother of three children.

BOB TUCKER

The Play's the Thing

Small Pieces of Soul, Back and Forth

Leah Olivier.
Pencil, 1996.

KEN: Hey Joey, he's stealin' home. You can get him.

JOEY: Comin' at ya, Ken.

KEN: Got'im by a mile. Hey Joey, how's your old man doin'
anyway? *Grounder to short. Can he turn the double play?*

JOEY: Got him at second, Ken. *And the throw to first . . . In time!*
He's still out of work. It's kind of weird having him around the
house all the time. He mostly mopes around and watches
television. When my mom gets home from work, he just yells
at her to make dinner. It's a drag. *Long fly ball to right field.
Ken goes way back to the wall and jumps for it . . .*

KEN: Got it, Joey. *The runner tags and goes home. The throw's
to the plate.*

JOEY: Got 'im! So Ken, they ever find that guy who hit your
little brother?

KEN: No. They found the stolen car, but they never found the
creep who hit him. *Seventh game of the World Series. Bottom of
the ninth. Bases loaded. Trying to hold a one-run lead. Works the
count to 3 and 2. The game rides on this one pitch. Here it comes.*

JOEY: *Striiiike!!! And the crowd goes crazy.* He ever gonna walk
again? *Here comes a hanging curve.*

KEN: Don't know. They're talking about another operation. *Smashes the hanging curve down the line . . .*

JOEY: *The third baseman leaps and grabs the line drive. What a play!* Must make ya kind of mad, huh? *And here's another curve ball . . .*

KEN: *Hey that one sunk. A stinker of a sinker.* No more curves Joey, okay? Yeah it makes me mad. But what can I do? Ya gotta go with the pitch, right? *High pop to shallow left . . .*

JOEY: *Charges in and makes the catch.* Hey did you see Miss Shumlin today? You could practically see right through her blouse. *This one's goin' over your head. Better go back for it . . .*

KEN: *Makes the over-the-shoulder catch. Just like a wide receiver.* You mean you could see her bra?

JOEY: Come on, Ken. You know Miss Shumlin doesn't wear a bra.

KEN: Oh yeah, how do *you* know?

JOEY: Everybody knows that!

KEN: Well I don't. How do ya tell?

JOEY: Open your eyes, Ken. If they jiggle, there's no bra. Come on, throw me the ball.

KEN: Oh yeah. *Here's the wind up. And the pitch. It's a fast ball.*

JOEY: *Yeah, a rising fast ball. Almost a wild pitch. Great save by the catcher.* You shoulda seen the dork she went off with after school.

KEN: Who?

JOEY: Miss Shumlin! *It's a scorcher to short . . .*

KEN: Ow! Hey Joey, take it easy. I don't have much padding left in this mitt. And what's with you and Miss Shumlin? You got a crush on her or something?

JOEY: Well I wouldn't mind putting the old squeeze play on her, if you know what I mean.

KEN: Joey?! She's a teacher!

JOEY: Oh I'm just kiddin'. I just can't figure out what a foxy lady like that is doin' with such a dork.

KEN: Maybe he's her brother?

JOEY: He put his arm around her and kissed her on the lips. That's no brother.

KEN: Oh, brother! Give it up, Joey. He's probably a nice guy, if Miss Shumlin likes him.

JOEY: But he's so ugly. Had pock marks all over his face. Gave me the creeps. Hey you gonna throw that ball or what?

KEN: Last throw. I gotta go. My mom's probably worried about me. Looks aren't everything, ya know.

JOEY: Oh yeah? Well tell that to my sister. All her friends are goin' out with boys, and she just stays in her room reading those stupid glamour magazines. Then, after we're all in bed, I hear her sneak down to the kitchen and eat . . . and eat . . . and eat. She just gets fatter and fatter.

KEN: Give me the ball. I really gotta go. It'll be okay, Joey. I bet it's just a phase she's goin' through. That's what my dad says about me after my mom and I go at it. I think Mom's the one goin' through a stage though, not me. Hasn't been the same since that damn accident. It's like she's always on me. Like she doesn't want to let me out of her sight.

JOEY: Well can you blame her? After what happened?

KEN: I don't know. It's just a pain.

JOEY: Hey Ken, see ya tomorrow.

KEN: Yeah, see ya. So they jiggle, huh? I'll watch for that.

JOEY: Want to come over after school? Bring your ball and mitt?

KEN: You bet. Nothing like tossin' the old ball around.

BOB TUCKER grew up playing catch on a narrow street on Long Island. When away from the office, he is a freelance entertainer, writing his own music and skits.

NAOMI GLADISH SMITH

Accidents Happen

Leah Olivier.
Pen-and-ink, 1996.

WHEN I REMEMBER MY CHILDHOOD, I recall those occasions when our games flirted with catastrophe. I also remember the manner in which mother handled our near disasters. What impresses me isn't just that she coped admirably with calamity, assessing the damage and taking appropriate action, but the fact that she didn't apportion blame. "Accidents happen," she'd say, and that would be that.

So we grew up figuring that if you weren't being unkind, you wouldn't be punished for something you had done, not even when—

as sometimes happened—you were the cause of carnage. Mother's philosophy of "Accidents Happen," however, must sometimes have been tried to the breaking point, for some of our games and the resulting mayhem bordered on the bizarre.

For a time we lived in a house located on a bank above the Kankakee River that had no running water except for that pumped up the hill from the river to flush the toilet. I remember it as an idyllic place. It didn't matter to us that we slept on a porch cold enough in winter to freeze the goldfish in their bowl. Even my brother Bob loved the place, despite the fact that he was the one who had to roll a dented milk can full of water for drinking and cooking from the neighbor's outdoor pump across a bumpy field to our house each day. The farmer neighbor whose pump we used let us explore his barn anytime we liked and let us play on an island he owned in the middle of the river.

It wasn't when leaping from the barn loft to the bails of hay beneath that we came to grief, or playing pirate among the high weeds and fallen trees of 'our' island, or even rowing a flat bottomed boat out into the river's uncertain currents. Trouble appeared in the form of a work gang that came to repair the road that ran between corn fields and sheep pastures.

One morning we kids watched, fascinated, as the crew of workmen broke up the asphalt. First one man would swing a pickax, then another would swing his in perfect, hypnotic rhythm, one ax flashing up at the same time the other flashed down. Thunk, thwack, thunk, thwack. The satisfying sounds were interrupted only when one of the men called a halt to lean on his ax and mop his face. At noontime the men dropped their tools and went off behind the barn to eat their sandwiches, and it was then that Bob told my sister Sylvia about the great idea he'd thought of. They could enlarge the hole the men had been working on; it wouldn't be so much play as helping the men out. Syl, flattered to be asked, didn't hesitate to head for a pickax.

The rhythm that looked so easy when the workmen did it, however, was actually a maneuver requiring split-second timing, an exercise as intricate as a minuet. I'm not sure how a scrawny thirteen-year-old boy or his even scrawnier ten-year-old sister even managed to hoist those pickaxes, but they did. And they got in a few satisfactory thunks before Syl didn't lift her head in time and the long, narrow point of Bob's descending ax caught the side of Sylvia's head.

According to family legend, only the bobby pins Syl wore in her hair saved the day. But for those bobby pins deflecting the ax, the story goes, I might have had to step in as a permanent backup in my brother's endless games of catch.

As it was, the ax did plenty of damage. Syl cried out and lurched off across the field, her hand clutching a head already streaming with blood. Bob ran beside her, worried but insisting that it really wasn't so bad. Surely she'd be fine if she just let him wrap something around it. Did she really have to go and tell mother?

Not stopping to debate the point Sylvia made a beeline for the house, staggering into the living room in one of the most dramatic entrances ever, as she trailed what seemed to be gallons of gore.

From the way mother handled it, you wouldn't have guessed that we hadn't a car and were three miles from the nearest doctor. She assessed the damage, cleaned Syl's head, and after bandaging the wound tightly, put her to bed for the rest of the day. And that was that. If mother was worried about the distance between us and the doctor, we didn't know it. Once mother realized no permanent injury had been done, she did the best she could and then simply kept a careful eye on her injured child.

And Bob was right. It really *wasn't* so bad, and Sylvia *was* fine. Of course Bob caught it for not taking care of his sister (a piece of disobedience right up there with nearly killing her), but mother was far more annoyed with the workmen than with Bob or Syl. The men should have known enough, she said, to put their tools away and not leave them around for children to play games with.

NONE OF US EVER touched a pickax again, but a few years later I did something remarkably similar when carried away with a chore I'd transformed into a game. And since I was the one at fault this time, mother's non-judgmental way of handling disaster impressed me even more.

By now we'd moved from the country to the city, and, in our new neighborhood, it was common to see house proud Scandinavian wives hang their carpets over a back-yard clothesline and beat the bejabbers out of the rugs with a little curlicued wire-fan beater. One day I was given the job of cleaning the porch rug and decided I'd bypass the vacuum cleaner and try it the neighbor ladies' way. We did not have one of those fan-shaped things, but with a twelve-year-old's ingenuity I figured a broom would do as well. I draped the carpet over the clothesline and swung away. Thwack! Thwack! It was fun. It was more than fun, it was eminently satisfying. I was a sword slashing adventurer; I was a masked avenger foiling a tyrant's evil plans. I might have finished with nothing more than a threadbare rug except for the fact that my six-year-old sister wandered across the yard and peeked out from behind the carpet just as I took a full force swing.

The metal top of the broom smacked both the carpet and Peggy's head, and my little sister fell, poleaxed, a white gaping gash above her left eye. I screamed for mother, and she came running. She hauled Peggy inside to put a cloth over a wound that by now was bleeding profusely, bleeding so much that Peggy couldn't see and thought she'd been blinded. And I, watching aghast and helpless, feared she was right.

While a neighbor took mother and Peggy to the doctor (we still didn't have a car), I sat on the front steps and waited, hot, anxious, and miserable. A small eternity later mother and Peggy returned, my sister's head swathed in bandages that covered a whole lot of stitches. Another hard-headed Gladish had survived.

The agonizing period when I sat on the front steps waiting to hear if Peggy was all right remains with me to this day, but I also remember that the minute mother took over, the horror eased. When at last they came home from the doctor's and my bandaged sister got out of the neighbor's car, an enormous weight lifted from me. The world righted itself because, dreadful as it had been, tragic as it almost was, I wasn't made to feel that I was at fault. Mother knew I hadn't intended any harm.

At the time I was only aware that mother was a good person to have around in an emergency; years later I realized that because mother accepted the fact that "accidents happen," I was able to do so too. The phrase comforted me then; it comforts me now. And, when I look back on it, I realize mother may have said it not just for our benefit, but for her own. Nobody's perfect, and nothing's one-hundred percent safe. When bad things happen, you do the best you can and don't worry about apportioning blame. I learned that there are consequences to be faced—Peggy still has a hairline scar and I'll never forget that anxious hour of sitting alone, waiting. But in the end, as mother said, "Accidents happen," and mostly we survive them, and, hopefully, learn from them.

NAOMI GLADISH SMITH is a Chicago area writer whose essays have appeared in *The Christian Science Monitor, The Journal of the American Medical Association,* and other publications.

CORRINE DE WINTER

The Rapture of Starfish

A broken starfish becomes,
in the course of time
two new ones.
No loss or memory of loss
although equipped
with a collection of eyes.

The rapture, the healing
of starfish
in the middle of so much blue
is remarkable.

They are used to growing miracles.
They are used
to reaching out
and finding what they need.

No one ever told them
they are merely husks
that were shed
from the burning stars above.

CORRINE DE WINTER has lived in Massachusetts all her life. Her poetry has been published in *Common Journeys* and *Ellipsis*.

M. GARRETT BAUMAN

Vacation with Family

WHEN FEBRUARY SNOW piles up on our window sills, my wife starts planning our summers on New England beaches. If Noah's wife had as much time to get ready, the ark wouldn't have floated. The night before our trip to Chatham, my family stands in the drive like waifs at the emigration docks with their worldly goods piled around them: one wife (Carol) and four kids.

"One bag and one suitcase each," I remind them. "No Barbie townhouses, no bicycles."

"One bag and one suitcase," Diana announces.

"Not a Hefty bag! And that's a steamer trunk."

Jeremy has a duffel bag stuffed to resemble Mike Tyson's punching bag. He can't lift it. It contains his rock collection. Cindy, meanwhile, tosses items into the trunk like a dock worker loading cod. "Cease!" I order magnificently. I'm iron. We almost have the station wagon stuffed when Carol reminds me she's hauling along an ice chest of food. To save twenty dollars we drag along an 80-pound monster which will slop icy water containing pickles and half-dissolved mayonnaise. To help find room, she digs for contraband. "What's this?"

"My fishing pole and tackle box," I say. She clicks her tongue. "They won't fit in a bag," I add.

"Oh? And this?"

"Well. The sombrero keeps me from getting sunburned. If I burn, I'll make everyone miserable."

"You look like grandma's floor lamp in it," she says, frisbeeing it over my outstretched arms to a kid who whisks it away.

Opposite:
Amy Gardner.
Vacation with Family.
Charcoal on bristol
board, 15×20 inches,
1996.

Jeremy cries. He can't decide if Curious George or the Teddy has to stay home. He makes them hug, then hands over lucky George.

After packing, the kids are too excited to sleep. Amy cries, Jeremy entertains us by sucking air from a mostly empty bottle, then pulling loose with a slurpy POP! One time the vacuum sucks his tongue into the bottleneck. He gurgles and flails arms. "Ih ont let oo!"

"Imagine if it never came off," Amy says.

"He'd have to eat through a straw," Cindy says.

"Up his nose," Diana adds.

"Onony's onna uut angy draw up ma ose."

"Come on," I say, leading Jeremy by the bottle.

"Ooh! Uhh! Uhh!" His eyes resemble firecrackers, and he waves his hands like a referee signaling time out. When he twists away, his red tongue squeezes out.

But that isn't the last we hear from Jeremy. Carol and I bed down our four pistons past midnight, and they run out of fuel by 1 AM. An hour later, Jeremy's crying wakes us. He's rolled over on a wad of baseball chewing gum, and the pillow's stuck to his hair. It takes nearly an hour to cut him loose.

The alarm rings at 4:30 and six zombies stumble downstairs towards our front door. "Somebody threw something in the john," Diana says.

Cindy says. "I thought it was a dead rat."

"That's Jeremy's hair and gum," Carol tells them.

"Ahh!" They scream at the sight of his ragged head. "Don't let him sit with us at the beach!"

We then hold the ritual farewell to the four cats after piling the cat food bags up where my neighbor can't miss them. Each kid kisses each cat. Whiskered faces are held to my lips, but I know the places those faces have been. I tap my foot and stare at the clock, but no one pays attention.

In the car—now 6 AM—the kids aren't sleeping as planned. They rock the car singing, "Plop! Plop! Fizz! Fizz! Oh what a relief it is!" That lasts a mile. Then they start, "Milk, milk, lemonade, round the corner fudge is made," using appropriate hand signals.

They're not hoarse for fifty miles. That's when my wife asks quietly, as if it's a passing thought, if the girls are sure they turned off their curling irons. Of course they did, I think. They've forgotten 999 of 999 mornings of their lives. The odds are in favor of them remembering. The dumb, long-haired cat likes warm things. She might lie on the curling irons and turn them off. Or, she might catch fire and run tearing around and burn the place to cinders. This is what vacations are for—to develop a devil-may-care attitude.

Later in the day I glance out my side window, and a woman in the passing car sticks her tongue at me. She puts her thumbs in her ears and gives me "moose wings" and a big grin. I elbow Carol. "I saw it," she says without moving her mouth.

A few cars later an old woman gives us a puckered dirty look. "Did you wash off the kid's graffiti on the car?" Carol asks. I had. Then a car with kids passes. They have noses and lips pushed against the side windows and slide their tongues around the glass like slugs. "Can you believe some parents allow . . ." I interrupt myself to check the mirror. Diana has pencils in both nostrils and Amy has stretched her upper lip up over her nose. The youngest chips in with obscene gestures. When the kids were younger, I used to draw maps of the United States so each time they spotted a new license plate, that state could be colored in. I thought it all-American. Until Jeremy swore he read an "Alaska" across the six-lane whizzing past at 60 miles per hour and a "California" passing on an overhead ramp. After that the game became cutthroat cheating and arguing. Anyone who's taken a family vacation knows what really counts is who did what to whom, how many times, and why.

We're red-eyed that night as we pull into a motel *with a pool*. When motels have pools, Carol and I collapse in the room and inhale the silence while the kids splash and scream in someone else's ears. We've been known to tip lifeguards. Tonight, however, Cindy and Amy return after an hour.

"Finished already?" I ask.

"Yeah," Cindy says. "Diana threw up in the pool."

"Is she all right?"

"Sure. We had the whole pool to ourselves after that," Amy says.

"How long ago did this happen?"

They shrug. Cindy says, "It started to spread around too much in the water, so we decided to come back."

Carol stares at me. I stare at her.

THE NEXT MORNING when I pull into our vacation hideaway in Chatham, it's tough not to recall those few vacations Carol and I shared alone. Would anyone seeing us in Burger King sucking acrylic milk shakes from paper cups with four kids ever believe we once shared romantic dinners in candlelit cafes where food comes without ketchup? Would anyone at the beach in Eastham watching a man who droops over his swim suit and who wipes sand from a crying kid's popsicle believe I went skinny-dipping? If I ever told the kids, "Fifteen years ago your mother and I made out right there on the beach one night," they'd think it was as gross as pointing out to visitors the location of our septic tank.

But we don't suggest such things. We're responsible adults who set down rules of vacation organization. Before we hit the beach, the car must be emptied and clothes stowed. The kids whine and complain and make us feel older. Suddenly I decide not to be the stick-in-the-mud. I toss the suitcases through the cottage door, rip off my shirt, declare, "Last one in's a rotten MCDLT" and rush toward the water. I race through the cottages and onto the clacking boardwalk, knowing the kids will be gaining. I wallow across the beach like a winded rhino, trip on the steep drop-off at the water's edge, and stumble into the surf. Saltwater blinds me, and I'm half-drowned and freezing. But I'm first! "Whooee!" I clear my eyes to bask in my madcap win. But there are no kids, no wife. Just six or eight dignified adults staring down the longest noses I've ever seen. I wheeze to my feet—now just a flabby forty-year-old who's fallen in the Atlantic Ocean—and slither past the eyes to the cottage, where everyone has neatly stowed their gear—except me. "Shall we go to the beach?" Amy says. She has packed a beach bag with towels, lotion. sunglasses, etc.

"How about bayside?" I suggest. "The surf's rough."

We rarely have trouble with our rentals, but travelers should take vacation ads with a cup of salt. One cottage we rented in Maine for a month promised "on the beach." It was one and a quarter miles through mosquito-thick blueberries to the shore. "No houses between us and the ocean," the crusty landlady said. "You're on the beach." The kids nicknamed her Ben Franklin for her chiseled jaw and steel skin. When the water from the faucet came out rusty brown and there was no gas in the stove, she said, "Send the boy over to my place with a jug. The gas truck'll be here Monday. Barbeque grill's out back." Also out back to supervise our cooking were the mosquitoes. They were descendants of the ones used in filming *The African Queen*. When Carol hung out laundry or cooked, she took the four kids as bodyguards to flap the air with newspapers.

Vacations, I believe, should be instructive for children. Once we rented a cottage in Wellfleet, and a French-speaking Canadian girl who knew no English became our girls' constant companion. When we heard ours say "rouge" for "red," we thought, how educational! Later we learned they had translated every bodily function and dirty word so they could awe their friends and hoodwink their teachers. This year I have hopes for ecology education—we'll learn about seashore life cycles, pollution, respect for nature, preserving habitat. I buy a book on seaside ecology and read selections to mixed reviews.

"This is so boring," Amy says.

"What is?" Diana says. "Did somebody say something?"

But one day they drag two fifteen-pound horseshoe crab carcasses to "study" in the front yard. The crabs decompose organically, and inhabitants of other cottages make ecological comments about us.

After the kids assemble a pile of shells (which our lawn mower will eventually convert to shrapnel), I decide to show them a live clam. I hold it up explaining how it inhales sand and nutrient goodies and then blows them out its other valve like exhaust. They inspect the grey, bubbly edge.

"It's gross and slimy," Diana says.

Cindy says, "Can you scrape that thing out so we can have the shell—how long will it stink afterward?"

"This is a living creature," I say, involuntarily holding it closer. "Hath not a clam feelings and affections? When you cut, doth it not bleed?"

"They don't have blood," Amy says. "Bivalves don't even have brains."

"Scientific knowledge is fine," I say. "But I'm trying to teach you to care about the shells you gather—*that all life is precious.*" I place the clam on the wet sand to return to nature and live in peace. We step back and wait for it to burrow under with the next wave.

"It looks dead," Cindy says. Just then a big, Black-backed Gull swoops down, grabs the clam, and flies up and out toward the jetty. It circles once, and a grey speck drops toward the rocks.

"I see what you mean, Dad, " someone says.

We take a day trip to Sandwich and swim in the warm bay. The water's still and glassy, the beach deserted, and a gauzy morning mist is just lifting. The perfect day! But Cindy thinks she glimpses crabs, and soon a huddled mass of children refuse to enjoy one of nature's greatest days.

"Let's go shopping," the girls say.

"They're just little sand crabs," I say. "Those cute, egg-shaped things that dig in sand and don't bite."

"It was big, Dad," Cindy says.

I wade into warm, shallow water. "It's so beautiful," I coax. "Mmmmn. See. It's perfectly . . ." I don't recall the primal scream. I do remember the feel of the steel trap on my right big toe. I raise the foot out of the water, a pink and blue crab dangling from my bloody appendage. Carol says I smacked the creature against the water, and it decided not to drag me out to sea. She also reports that I left the water like a two-hundred pound duck trying to lift off from a pond. I thank her for having such a photographic memory. I thank her each time she recites the story for family gatherings.

At night, without television and without teenage boys honking for one's daughters, *people on vacations become families again.* With humidity-softened snacks, cheeks and arms aglow with sun, and a cool breeze blowing through the screen door, someone says, "Let's play a game." There're charades and poker (with kids smoking pretzel stogies and betting red chips by the handful), but for real togetherness our family plays *Life.* It started in Bar Harbor on a rainy day, and followed every night for three weeks that July. We bought insurance, paid for college educations and cars, had babies, and kept getting sent back to start. Sitting in a rain-pelted cottage with four kids, it seemed a bit redundant. Our game place-markers are plastic cars, and we load them with pink and blue pegs for babies as we drive around our lives. It's traditional. *Life* gets stashed in the station wagon each vacation. Carol says when she spots the little peg babies lying around the cottage, she vacuums each one up with a grin. Someday, I suppose. We'll miss them, but so far we haven't run out.

The last night while playing *Life,* I'm sent back to Start, broken financially with blue pegs when I finally approach the square labeled "Final Reckoning." I start to say a prayer that the real car will start tomorrow morning when we are to leave for home.

"Do we have to go?" Jeremy says.

"Yeah," another kid sighs. "Let's stay here forever."

"Your turn," Carol says and lays her hand over my fist. I smile and roll the dice.

M. GARRETT BAUMAN teaches English and human ecology at Monroe Community College, Rochester, New York. Home is in the rural Finger Lakes region. He received a New York State Fellowship for the Arts, has authored two books, and writes for *Fine Homebuilding, The New York Times, Orion, Yankee,* and other magazines.

PART III

Dark Corners under the Big Top

WITHOUT SHADOWS, WOULD WE KNOW LIGHT?

Is playing to win the only way to play?
Are there sadder words than, "I wish I had . . . ?"
Does the hero always hit a homer in the bottom
of the ninth, or does the home run always win the
game?

No? Then you may find the pieces in this
section the most memorable in the book. Play is not all
fun and games. Far more than games, play is the work
or diversion that we do in the spirit of play, a spirit
of risk and commitment and immersion which at its
best achieves what the mystic Swedenborg described
as the properly balanced approach to life.

More than fun, play includes the pinnacles
and chasms of human emotion. Players are
exhilarated, frustrated, elated, and heartbroken many
times in the course of a season, a tournament, even
a single game. Stories and recollections here are happy,
strange, lovely, and sad.

SEAN MACDONALD

The Voice

René Magritte. *Pandora's Box*. Oil on canvas, 30×26 inches, 1951. New Haven: Yale University Art Gallery. Gift of Dr. and Mrs. John A. Cook B.A. 1932 (1961.8).

MY MOTHER SHOOK ME AWAKE that night, and her salty tears fell on my face as she sobbed. "Antonio," she wailed. "Do you hear it? Tell me you hear it. It is the most beautiful voice I have ever heard!" She was slender and tall like a sunflower, wilting over me in agony. Her large eyes stared like a giraffe's. She seemed impaled on the high-pitched melody that pierced the air. The rolling sound ignited the essence of my mother, and as I listened, I could feel my nine-year-old heart trembling. That misty night the wolves were howling as if scared, and the full moon made shadows like goblins through the French doors of my bedroom.

I RAN INTO FRANÇOIS DU MONDE in late summer at a street side café in Florence. I had no trouble recognizing his pointed nose, his posture; he leaned over the square table with his hair covering his eyes like a sheepdog. He had the look of a man who had just battled a fierce war. It had been eleven years since I met him briefly during an official party at City Hall. We had barely exchanged words then, but on that sweltering day in August, he unfolded the vivid account of his love for Ada Magnanis and the death of this woman whose voice had transformed a nation.

His haunting story was not completely unfamiliar to me. I had first heard of him when my mother was sitting in the piazza that spring when I was nine. She was reading the newspaper and told me that the mayor's daughter, Ada, had acquired a new chauffeur after the old one lost his leg in a tractor accident. They announced the new driver as the stunning Frenchman who watched over the most beautiful models in Paris. He was a security guard, and suspected lover and rumored confidant of the famed Marie Clarie, until her fall from the runway spotlight. François was the envy of the people in Florence for his constant access to Ada, whose impassioned outbursts had captured the attention of the city.

When I met him in the café, François immediately purchased a coffee for me and held my hand across the table while he spoke. As he looked deeply into my eyes, he confessed his life to me. He explained that his character had been formed on the farmlands outside Lyon, where he and his brother continued the legacy of their deceased father's grape-growing. The vineyards had drawn celebrities from Paris who lured François, at the age of twenty-five, to the prestige of knowing the popular and eccentric in Paris.

This incipient desire for notoriety led him to the world of fashion, but a dispute between him and Jack Gordon, director of *Zam Magazine,* over a contract for a fashion model, ruined his career in the business. His love for models turned him into the "famous security guard." But persistent humiliation from the hot-shot insiders of the fashion world forced him out of Paris to the coast of the Riviera and finally to Florence and the bedside of Ada. This is where his real story began.

Upon his arrival in Florence, François was treated to an extravagant luncheon of roasted quail with the local dignitaries who explained the importance of his job. He was to guard and protect Ada for the crucial role she played to the city of Florence and to the world. Although François thought their investment in her exaggerated, he committed himself to care for her with grace and courage. They shook hands like members of a secret fraternal order. From there he went to his accommodations in the newly refurbished carriage house that he decorated with the prized antiques he had acquired in Paris. That afternoon, the smell of freshly varnished wood made him light-headed and he fell into a deep sleep.

While sleeping, he dreamt of the Virgin Mary appearing in divine light. She sang an aria of complete subtlety and magnificence beyond any sound he had heard before. As the beatific tones spread, her light emanated outward until everything was engulfed in it and he could distinguish no endings or beginnings or distinctions in time and space. She folded her blazing white hands at her chest, bowed to him, and vanished.

I had the impression that this experience marked the beginning of François's mystical journey. From that time on, he took moments to sit in silence and to reflect on his life, rather than shuffling from one event to the next as he was used to doing.

That night, François was introduced to Ada by Ercole Ricci, the stalwart vice-mayor who kept a picture of the mayor on his bedside table. Ada tried not to see anyone and lived a life of privacy and solitude. She looked like a wild angel with dark locks. He noticed her demeanor of complete humility as she stared steadily at the floor when the two men entered her enormous velvet-curtained room. But when Ricci left the chamber, she began laughing vehemently at nothing in particular. She stood up and circled François, moving ritually in her flowing green linen dress.

At this point in his story, the sun was setting, and the maitre d' was lighting candles on the tables in the dusty café. François du Monde removed a silver locket from around his neck and opened it to reveal the photograph of a striking woman whom I immediately recognized to be Ada. Her face was pale and round with soft puckered lips. But what was most engrossing about her was the fiery blue of her eyes which were set wide apart. These eyes had a fierce omniscience which I had never before witnessed. They penetrated me as if I were looking at a living person. I instantly lost myself in her presence. At that moment I understood the great enthusiasm which had always surrounded this gem of Florence. I also understood why she had been racked by the problems of clairvoyance; I had heard that Ada slipped into trances at the dinner table, often causing herself to tip back in her chair and fall violently onto the floor, where from her staff of servants, secretary, and security guard would quickly scoop her up with concerned eyes.

"I sat on a chair by Ada's bedroom door and tried to keep to myself," François resumed. "But I was constantly drawn to her behavior. She seemed to move from activity to activity in a spontaneity unrestrained by convention. She began hammering nails into a box painted sweet orange and then suddenly threw the hammer across the

room; it shattered a vase. She then raised herself like a swan flapping its wings against the water's surface and began dancing passionately in the center of the chandelier-lit room, oblivious to my presence. She was self-fulfilled and erotic in a beautiful way, not salacious at all. She continued like this, from dancing, to painting, to hammering, for the next two hours. She was a creative instrument who manifested beautiful repertories of music and postures almost unbe-

Max Ernst. *Paris–Revê*. Oil on canvas, 24×28 inches, ca. 1924. New Haven: Yale University Art Gallery. Bequest of Katherine S. Dreier to the Collection Société Anonyme (1952.30.5).

knownst to herself. They simply flowed out of her in an uncontrollable torrent of creativity."

François could not take his eyes off this sensation of a woman. He sat, dazzled by her, until she scooped up a handful of black soil from a potted plant and threw it violently in his face. At the moment the dirt made its impact, a most unusual event took place. The room and Ada dissolved into streams of iridescent light. Like rain sliding down a window pane, François's structured world melted. Pulses of ecstatic energy crawled up his arms like an army of hungry ants. He lost himself to an other-worldly place of complete freedom. He began floating through translucent waves of blue, red, and green lights and he could see other beings, exquisitely bright and formless, who jetted from one place to the next in record speed. Suddenly an odd force tugged at his buttocks. He was sucked back into the wooden chair and the mayor's mansion and the reality of Ada who was whirling ecstatically under the chandelier like a dervish.

He looked at his hands and legs in relation to the room in order to place himself. He felt dizzy and green. He swiftly staggered to Ada and grasped her shoulders to halt her spinning. "What have you done to me?" he said. He felt out of control. Ada looked at his knitted eyebrows and stern expression and smiled.

"I do nothing. You are a foolish man. I like you," Ada said.

François stared into her radiant eyes and realized that Ada possessed a freedom of spirit which was reflected in her highly focused but seemingly outrageous movements. She made him feel crazy. He let out an enormous breath, turned abruptly away from her, and walked quickly out of the room.

He woke up in the middle of that night to a high-pitched melody of extraordinary caliber. When he realized the sound was a human voice, he leapt out of bed to the window and peered into the fog, hoping to realize its source. Tears began rolling down his cheeks. He began shivering in an uncontrollable excitement. Closing his eyes, he let the music move him into a trance-like state. It suddenly dawned on him that the sound came from the bedroom of Ada.

He pressed his finger to the chilled pane of glass and pushed the window out over the garden. He leaned his muscular body out into the cold and glanced up to her candlelit window. He was certain that the voice came from there but he wondered how any human being could produce such piercing sounds. He had once heard Pavarotti in concert but what he was hearing now put even the opera star to shame. François closed the window, buried himself beneath the down comforter and thought intensely about the marvelous world he had entered and contemplated in wonder the impact this porcelain-faced woman would have on his life.

Over the next two years, François worked diligently for the mayor to secure a lifelong position as chauffeur. He fell in love with Ada and the mysterious way she cared nothing for the outside world. She refused to go to public functions like Carnival, especially since hundreds of city people had begun camping outside the grounds of the mansion. News had spread that it was Ada's voice people had heard over the years in the middle of the night. The town paper published the information when a jealous servant who imitated Ada's hairstyles leaked the secret. The servant was given 100,000 lira but people came to despise her because of the upset it caused Ada. In fact, people panicked the week that the voice was not heard in the middle of the night. François nursed Ada that week. She did not leave her bed.

Ada's vast talents in the arts, her craftsmanship and her athletic prowess, opened François's mind and gave him a vitality that he had not felt since he ran through the vineyards and played with wild birds and snakes as a child. He dreamt of her and felt fulfilled in her presence. The tenacious rumble in his stomach was his fear to be alone and without her power.

One morning, when spring was becoming summer, the mayor stormed into Ada's room. The gluttonous man with enormous belly and slicked-back silver hair commanded Ada in his deep scratchy voice to sit down. "The city is out of control. The people insist on a performance from you, and with the election in two months, I must do everything in my power to appease the citizens of this fine city. You will perform this Saturday evening outdoors in the Royal Pavilion at 8 o'clock. I do not want any trouble from you. I have given you everything a daughter could want, and I expect that you will satisfy your father this one time."

Ada slid the brass lock of her door closed and refused to admit anyone for the days which followed, anyone except her confidant, François du Monde, who was anxious. She placed her red lips against the door and smeared her face paints across the panel as she screamed to her father, "I will not sing for anyone." She paced around the room. "It will be my death," she murmured as if she could prophesy something that no one else understood. She and François ate assortments of meats and cheeses delivered by the dumbwaiter and contemplated plans for action during those blistering days. That Friday night while François slept on the floor of the bathroom wrapped in Ada's fuzzy white bathrobe, he dreamt vividly of Ada placing her lips on his. In the morning as he stared at the velvet curtains, François remembered the hotel rooms of Paris and the romance he associated with them. He had been in love like this before, and that same eerie fear settled into his aging bones as he thought of Jack Gordon and the collapse of his burgeoning enterprise for the price of love. He knew the mayor would be upset to have the chauffeur locked in his daughter's room for three days only to come out and say that she will not perform. His job relied on her performance and he could not bear the thought of not being with her every day.

He asked Ada, "Why don't you perform, my sweet?"

She ignored his question and continued the knitting of a scarf which was now forty-three feet long. Trying to discern her mood, he put on an audio cassette of *Bolero*. Tears streamed down Ada's face as her hands spun like the wheels of a locomotive, the needles stitching faster than a sewing machine. "If you do not perform, I will lose my job. I cannot live without you," sighed François du Monde.

Ada's blue eyes focused on the dancing needles. They stayed that way for hours. The sun lowered itself through the clouds to make shadows stretch and the reds of the sky come to life. Obsessive townspeople began chanting her name and he could hear their echo off the mansion walls. Cars sped past the windows, horns honking meaningfully and enthusiastically. One could imagine the Italian disco music blaring in them with greasy teenagers singing along. François became frightened and asked if Ada needed anything, but she did not respond. She knitted until he saw the last piece of yarn collect itself into the never ending scarf. When it vanished like a mouse's tail under a door's crack, the knitting needles stopped and Ada looked up. "I will sing. For you, I will sing," she said in a somber voice, the memory of which made François shake as he spoke the words to me.

Moments before Ada was to make her entrance, the thousands who were packed into the outdoor stadium grew silent. It was the frightening silence that occurs in the interval between the cries of animals on a dark forest night. As Ada graced the stage in her black silk dress, the crowd could not help but come to their feet. They were silent and awestruck. Lavender lights set her aglow but it was her conscious steps and glaring stare which halted all noise so that only the wind's whisper against the back of necks could be sensed. The masses sat down and a single spotlight illuminated Ada's ivory skin. Her eyes lifted to face the crowd, her lips separated, and a faint-sounding murmur aggrandized itself, from pianissimo to fortissimo in an instant, then split the air like an aircraft breaking the sound barrier. Her body writhed in ecstasy as a mellifluous aria overflowed from her lips.

People in the crowd burst into emotional fits of crying, screaming, and moaning as a result of the powerful vibration of music which emanated from the petite woman. Her voice became so overwhelming that the people covered their ears and looked at their feet to avoid the intensity. She was in solitude now except for the one olive-skinned spectator who writhed as she did. His eyes were to her face. His ears were to her melody. And as François du Monde listened, in joy which penetrated the marrow of his bones, he remembered his origins as heaven's light.

The aria grew increasingly louder, and although the crowd could not bear its volume except through the muffle of their hands, François gave his body and soul over to the music. His soul nude to her rapture, François witnessed the swirling clouds above Ada and then the sudden appearance of a flock of wild birds who circled her. They squawked around her, excited. Lightning burst forth from behind the clouds, lighting the terrified faces of the hovered lovers of music, the seekers who could not bear the freedom of Ada's expression. Thunder rumbled like angry gods beating drums. She was ecstatic and only François had the strength and courage to bear her force.

François remembered nothing else of that night. Three days later, he woke up in a hospital where doctors told him he had fallen into a coma. They had taken him from the pavilion to the emergency room on the night of the performance. When he came to, his friends from the mayor's mansion had to show him a copy of the daily newspaper to prove that Ada had died. He was weary from the medications he had been given. He was numb to the fierce pain in his heart. The report explained that after two hours of singing, the magical woman of Florence held a high note for nearly fifteen minutes.

When she collapsed, the note ended. She was rushed to the hospital where nervous doctors did all they could to start the pulsing rhythm of her heart. It was not easy for François to believe that the one he loved was no more.

It had grown dark, but the heat was still oppressive. I recalled that I had come to the piazza to go shopping. People swarmed around me, beggars, artists on the corners painting, but I was conscious only of the sticky perspiration that layered itself on my skin. I was uncomfortable and self-absorbed, but somehow aware that I needed to be wrapped in myself right then in order to function. I had no idea that my entrance into the café for an icy gellati would lead to my engagement with François du Monde. I did not quite know how to reenter the world I had left only a few hours before.

SEAN MACDONALD is a graduate student at the University of Wisconsin where he studies South Asian religions. His primary interests include friendship, travel, holistic health, and the perennial philosophies of the East.

DAVID DEBELLIS JONES

The Day the Babe Called His Shot Again

Harold E. Edgerton. *Baseball Swing No. 1.* Black-and-white photograph, detail. Concord, Massachusetts: Palm Press, Inc. Harold E. Edgerton 1992 Trust.

THAT DAY STARTED OUT like any typical July day in the East, mild weather in the morning, but by noon the temperature had soared to 95 degrees with the humidity so high that catching your breath was almost as hard as catching a Nolan Ryan fastball. I decided to go to a Yankee game, opting to go by myself because I had some serious thinking to do. I had applied to Georgetown Law School that spring, but I was having second thoughts about going if I was accepted. My dream was to play professional baseball even though I hadn't been drafted into the pros while playing shortstop at Michigan State.

As I drove to Yankee Stadium, I tried to sort things out, but the more I thought about what I ought to do, the more confused I became. I didn't want to disappoint my father, who had my life planned out for me: first law school, then a junior partner in his law firm, then full partnership; on the other hand, I felt I should be true to my own desires, whatever they were, because, when you're part of a close-knit family, you sometimes have trouble distinguishing what *you* want from what your parents want *for* you.

By the end of the sixth inning, the Yanks were ahead of the Boston Red Sox, 1 to 0. Not much exciting had happened except for a home run by Don Mattingly. Then, as the fans settled into their seats after the seventh-inning stretch, a strange and unearthly silence came over Yankee Stadium. The air was filled with some sort of weird static electricity, as if pins and needles were dancing in the air. I was looking at my program to see who was coming to bat for the Yankees. When I looked up, I was shocked by what I saw and heard.

The announcer came over the public address system. The deep and hollow voice that seemed to come from some place faraway said, "The batter is Babe Ruth." That's when a ghostly entourage appeared on the field, one player for each position. The figures were transparent but had just enough outline to be clearly visible.

Up to the plate strode Babe Ruth. Even as an apparition, there was no mistaking him, that baby face, the pot belly, the spindly legs, those ballet-like ankles, the barrel chest, that unique batting stance with his feet placed close together. The Babe took a couple of practice swings and stood ready. The phantom pitcher wound up and tossed the first pitch. Ruth let it go. After a ghostly umpire called a strike, Ruth lifted one finger as if to say, "That's strike one." After two balls, the fourth pitch was also called a strike. The Babe held up two fingers as if to say, "That's strike two." He gestured, then, at the center-field grandstand, indicating he'd hit the ball there on the next pitch.

That's when I realized what I was seeing. The fifth inning of the fourth game of the 1932 World Series between the Yankees and the Cubs, when Babe Ruth called his shot against Charlie Root in Chicago. Ruth had been really steamed up that day. Bench jockeys for the Cubs were riding him unmercifully, and Chicago fans were peppering him with lemons from the stands.

Root delivered the next pitch, and the Babe hit a tremendous home run into the center-field stands. I watched enthralled as Ruth rounded the bases with those mincing steps, doffing his cap to the fans, his moon face aglow, the piano legs churning, taking his time, enjoying every moment of his glory. As he crossed home plate, he vanished, as did the other phantom players, and everything was as before, the low murmur of the crowd in my ears, a woman near the aisle taking an ice cream bar from a vendor, the vendor continuing on up the aisle shouting, "Ice cream. Get your ice cream."

I felt lightheaded and ecstatic, and my flesh crawled with goose bumps. My awe was soon replaced by curiosity. Had anyone else seen what I had? What did it mean? The couple next to me, upwardly mobile types in their late twenties, were discussing where to go for dinner. The middle-aged man in the row in front of me was cautioning his two kids not to lean over the rail if a foul ball came their way. The fan to my left was an old man wearing a Yankee cap. He was lost in thought, the only candidate around me who could have seen what I had.

"Excuse me," I said. "Did you just see something unusual?"

"Like what?" he said, his eyebrows raised.

When I didn't answer, he shrugged and turned his attention to the playing field.

Later, as I was leaving the game, I saw a kid who lived down the block from me in Greenwich. Bobby was ahead of me, walking down the ramp toward an exit with his father by his side. Bobby Groiner was ten years younger than I, about twelve years old, tall for his age, a nice kid who loved the great American pastime as much as I did. Almost every time I saw him, he was wandering off somewhere pounding a hardball into his glove.

ON THE DRIVE HOME I listened to the radio for any mention of the apparitions. I heard only the score and the usual details of a baseball game. Had I seen a vision? If so, what did it mean? Or was it a hallucination, the product of too many beers and too much hot sun? Then, again, perhaps I had seen ghosts. Maybe the spirits of departed Yankees returned to Yankee Stadium to relive their moments of glory. These questions buzzed around inside of me like a swarm of bees trying to get out.

When I arrived at home, my mother's voice was filled with excitement. "Jeff, a letter came today from Georgetown Law School."

I opened it and scanned the contents. "I've been accepted," I said, my eyes downcast.

"What's the matter?" she asked. "This is wonderful news!"

"I've changed my mind about law school."

"I . . . I don't understand," she said, confused. "Your father will be terribly upset."

"I want to play professional baseball."

"But I thought . . ."

"There's someone I need to talk to, Mom, I'll be back in time for dinner."

I rushed out the front door and hurried down the street toward the Groiner residence, keeping my eyes peeled for Bobby. He was tossing a baseball in the air in his back yard, playing pitch and catch with himself.

"Hi, Bobby," I shouted.

"Hey, Jeff," he called back.

"Can I talk to you?"

"Sure," he said. "You want to toss the ball around?"

"Okay," I said. "You got a glove I can use?"

He was in and out his backdoor in a flash, a catcher's mitt in his free hand. "I'll pitch and you catch," he said, tossing me the mitt. "What d'ya want to talk about?"

"I saw you at the Yankee game this afternoon. What I want to know is, did you see, um, anything unusual?"

He blinked rapidly a few times, then said guardedly, "Maybe I did and maybe I didn't."

"You *did* see something," I said, a wild hope surging through me.

"What'd *you* see?" he said, his eyes wide with wonder. "You first!"

"I saw Babe Ruth call his shot," I said.

Bobby jumped in the air. "I thought I was the only one who saw it! I wasn't sure if I imagined it or what."

"Did your father see it?"

"Nobody did that I know of except you and me."

"Did you tell your father what you saw?"

"Yea," he said dejectedly. "He said he wouldn't take me to any more games if I made things up."

"What do you think it means, Bobby?"

"I don't know," he said. "What do *you* think?"

"I wish I knew."

I walked ninety feet away, the distance from the pitcher's mound to home plate, crouched down behind an imaginary plate, and said, "Okay, Bobby, show me your stuff."

The kid let loose with a curve ball that broke so sharply it made me blink. "That's a great curve. You've got a good arm."

"Want to see another one of my pitches?"

"Okay."

That's when he threw me a wicked screwball, the pitch moving down and away so much it popped out of my glove. "Great pitch," I said. "What else you got?"

He threw me a knuckleball that dropped so steeply it looked like a ball rolling off the top of a table. "You're good, kid," I told him. "Real good."

"I'm going to pitch for the New York Yankees."

"Don't let go of that dream, kid."

My dream was to play for the Yankees, too. Baseball is the only thing I've ever loved. I played sandlot as a kid, went on to play American Legion ball, starred on my high school team, and batted over .300 at Michigan State, where I didn't hit with much power, which is probably why I wasn't drafted by the pros. Not getting a pro bid was the biggest disappointment of my life, but I knew I could still make it to the "bigs" if I impressed someone at a Yankee tryout camp. One was coming up in two weeks.

Bobby Groiner threw me a lot more pitches, knuckle curves, sliders, palm balls, fast balls, change-ups, you name it, and he threw them all with a windup that concealed his intentions and with a control that belied his years. I left for home that day without saying anything more to him about what we'd both seen at Yankee Stadium. After all, what more *was* there to say?

My father called me into his study as soon as I returned home. He stared at me with disappointment for a long time and then began to pace back and forth as I'd seen him do when he summed up a case before a jury. "Your mother told me you've decided against going to law school," he said.

"I want to play professional ball, Dad."

"I thought that dream died when you weren't drafted into the pros."

"I can still make it at a tryout camp."

"The odds of making it to the majors are a thousand to one," he countered as he continued to pace. "These days even the most promising players spend four or five years in the minors. If you were anyone else, I'd say give it a try, but you're in a unique position, son. When you graduate from Georgetown, you'll step right into the family firm. Do you know how many young men and women would give their right arm for an opportunity like that?"

I had to admit he was right, but I countered with, "If I don't make it to the bigs, I can go to law school later."

He shook his head. "You have things backwards, son. The time to finish your education is now. If you don't go to law school now, you may never go. Time has a way of getting away from you. Get your education first so you'll have a skill to fall back on."

My father then painted a glowing picture of the life I'd lead as a member of his law firm. He talked for a long time about how I'd have money up the wazoo, be up to my elbows in pretty women, drive brand new cars, be a respected member of my community, and own a beautiful home, all of which I admit had great appeal.

"My dream is to play for the Yankees," I said when he'd finished. "I once told you that."

"Son, that's not a dream, that's a pipe dream. Don't throw your life away on a pipe dream. You'll regret it to your dying day. Since you're being so pigheaded, maybe we can compromise. I'll tell you what. Finish your first year of law school. Do that for me. Then, if you still want to try pro ball, you can do so with my blessings."

My first year at Georgetown Law was a real yawner. It was all I could do to keep from falling asleep in class. I did well in my studies, though. I suppose what I learned was that I'm a Jenson after all, born and bred for the law like my father, even if I'm less enthusiastic about the subject than he. I hadn't given up on playing pro ball, though. I still intended to give it a try as soon as summer arrived.

In April of that year I met Susan Shriner. She was an undergraduate at Georgetown majoring in political science, and her father was a judge. We hit it off right away, and by June we were engaged. I didn't want to get married right away, but she insisted. I didn't want children right away either, but Susan got pregnant a month later, and I became the father of a son. I kept telling myself I'd go to that Yankee tryout camp after I graduated from law school, but by that time our second child, a girl, was on the way. The day after I graduated, I went to work for my father.

I READ ABOUT BOBBY GROINER TODAY in the sports section of *The New York Times*. He made the starting rotation for the Yanks and is a candidate for Rookie of the Year. I often think about that day ten years ago when Bobby and I saw Babe Ruth call his shot again, and I still wonder what it meant. Maybe I'll call Bobby one of these days and ask him; I think he's figured it out.

DAVID DEBELLIS JONES, a writer living in Pennsylvania, has recently been published in *Spitball* magazine.

PEGGY NORTH–JONES

What We Remember

Joan Miró. *The Family.*
Vine charcoal, white
pastel, and red conté on
oatmeal paper, 41×29¼
inches, 1924. New York:
The Museum of Modern
Art. Photograph 1996.
Gift of Mr. and Mrs.
Jan Mitchell.

I have been a family therapist and family educator for twenty-five years and a widow for ten months now. Having spent countless hours in undergraduate and graduate classes, internships, and in clinical practice, it seems ironic to feel that I have learned more about interpersonal relationships in the last year than I have during my entire professional life. Death teaches vibrantly clear lessons by simplifying, by stripping away the frivolous, confusing distracters. How paradoxical it feels to have learned a potent lesson about one aspect of relationships—play—as a result of experiencing the death of my husband.

IN MY WORK WITH FAMILIES, we solve problems, and we work on communication and mutual respect. Toward the end of therapy, I always try to focus on the importance of having fun as a family; we talk about how families get so caught up in the busyness and crises of life in general that they forget to celebrate the special meaning of their own families. I encourage family members to laugh, to have fun together, to be silly, to play. But only in the last six months have I begun to truly understand that while the hard work families do is important, playfulness may be one of the most critical areas to explore and to recommend early in the treatment process.

For my own family, my husband Dan's illness and death were unmercifully fast. My children and I had only five months to absorb a diagnosis, watch a dramatic struggle with cancer, and accept that the man we loved so much was gone before we had time even to understand what was happening.

One sunny Friday in May, he went for his annual required physical, completed all the necessary specialty tests, and took the rest of the day off to play golf, a relaxing start to a three-day weekend. He had done this exact same thing for the last five years. On Monday, he received a phone call from the doctor's office indicating there were some problems with the chest x-ray, and he needed to go to the medical center for a repeat test. We were fairly nonchalant, not giving it much thought, and he went alone to the hospital Tuesday morning.

I was with my first patient of the morning when he called. I still remember the chilling words "it doesn't look good. There are spots on my lungs and they are sending me for a CAT scan. Please call Dr. Grant and see what you should do. I have to go. They're waiting for me."

Dr. Grant took my phone call immediately and asked me to please meet him and my husband at his office in the next hour. I dropped everything and left my office. Things were never to return to normal again.

What followed in the next few weeks was a valiant effort to stop the invasive spread of a renal cell carcinoma. We went through diagnostic tests, decision-making and consultation with specialists, interferon and chemotherapy, radiation, and surgery to replace shattered bones as the cancer spread to the bone, and finally, to the painful acceptance and move into a hospice program.

In the end, the cancer's impact on, and transformation of, this robust, healthy, never-ill man was so complete that dying, even though we did not want to let him go, seemed his only source of peace and freedom from pain. Coping with the illness and the treatments and just making it through the hours of the day—to see if maybe tomorrow would bring "the break he just couldn't catch," he'd say—consumed all his energy.

What I see so clearly, ten months later, was that he could no longer laugh, or enjoy, or play, and every waking moment was hard, hard work for each of us. Every move seemed incredibly exhausting physically. We spent hours moving with a walker, trailing oxygen tanks and tubing. Dressing, bathing, eating, and just going into the bathroom were long, tedious tasks for him and for the family member or friend who became a necessary partner to help accomplish these tasks. Even sleeping, which he had always loved ("what could be more wonderful than a long nap on vacation? Forget the sightseeing!" he would say to tease me, as I sat armed with guide books of every description) became frightening, frequently interrupted, and a difficult task which he struggled to achieve through the long hours of darkness each night.

When I think of Dan in those weeks and days, the memory of the physical transformation is overwhelming. It is not the face or the image of the man that I loved and spent twenty-two years with that surfaces amidst the tears of painful mourning. So, I quickly search my memory for something more bearable—something both lighter and more substantial, that I can hold onto and gain some measure of comfort from. What I find are always images of Dan playing. I thank goodness I can retrieve those memories easily. So evidently can everyone else, for that is what we all seem to remember best about him. He loved to play!

Dan did not play frequently, maybe not even often, but, when he did, it was evident he was *really* having fun. Growing up, his family took only one vacation—to Arkansas to visit his mother's friend—but for us, vacations became a serious mental-health investment for two weeks every summer and, more recently, for another week in the spring. The last two vacations we took were especially wonderful and left us filled with reminiscences of places and things deserving an encore, which we assumed we'd soon enjoy.

On our long trek west last summer, with my sister and her husband and children, Dan was in his element pretending to be a cowboy! In Wyoming, he found the perfect cowboy hat—wide-brimmed, black suede with a multicolored ribbon—and luxuriated in wearing it on several trail rides. He tolerated our kidding and teased back at his son and daughter as they literally rode away into the sunset to a cowboy cookout and campfire. We treasure the memories and the images of those two weeks out west with Dan tanned and beaming and as healthful-looking as I had ever seen him. Thank goodness we took this time to play!

Charles M. Russell.
Bucking Bronco. Oil on
canvas, 10×20 inches,
1904. Tempe: Arizona
State University Art
Museum (52.128). Gift
of Oliver B. James.

The last trip we took together was at a time when everyone had had enough of the gloomy days of late winter. There Dan with one of his best buddies was able to golf until he had his fill. It comforts me that his passion for golf grew so fervently in his last two years. Whenever things were getting intolerable at work, or when everyone needed a break, he seemed to be the one who would call the guys together, take a day or a half-day off, and head for the golf course. He became so interested in the sport that he bought a ridiculous Panama hat to play in, the necessary equipment, and would even make a game out of shining and cleaning the soft leather shoes, florescent orange balls, and personalized tees so that he was always ready. His skill evidently left much to be desired, but he loved to play *at* golf. And play he did!

On these vacations when the hours on the links were over, he would return and relax on the beach, which might include tossing a football to his son and his friends—a lasting, important memory they say, for them. It was not always a football game, but just a chance for a father and his son and son's buddies to fool around and have fun.

At Dan's memorial celebration, friends and family members shared their memories from different parts of his life. Each involved playing. One childhood friend recalled cruising the strip in their small Illinois town on weekend nights looking for fun, his current buddies shared their golf "war stories," and close family friends told of their daughters announcing Dan was "cool" when he blared the radio in his midlife-crisis-sports-car every time the song *Turn the Radio Up with the Good Songs* came on. His older sister recalled the hand-picked "special birthday cards" he sent aimed at reminding her, not so gently, of her rapidly advancing age; and his younger sister reminisced about how he tortured her with seemingly unending tickle bouts until she would yell "uncle." And all recalled the silly, playful grin Dan put on at these times. I am so glad that he had fun while he could!

WHAT IF WE HAD NOT PLAYED? What if we had been so caught up in ourselves, our careers, or in materialistic pursuits that he had not coached the girls' softball team at that ridiculous pre-adolescent stage where they cried and bickered about everything from the way their shirts fit to their hairdos being messed up by the batting helmet, when they needed a referee more than a coach? Or what if he had not coached the boys' baseball team where hours were spent teaching lessons on how to control one's temper on the diamond? What if he had never worn his cowboy hat nor included us in his Hop-a-long Cassidy fantasy? What if he had not created endless laughter by drumming on the steering wheel in his sports car to the latest pop song, always heavily in tempo?

If we hadn't watched him play and played with him, the memories left would not be so bearable. Those remembrances soften and dull the edges of the terribly sharp pain that is here every day. Some of my last memories are of painful, arduous walks, and eventually wheelchair rides to the car to attend daily sessions of radiation. But, even in those final days, on Friday afternoons, with everyone's help, Dan donned his high school baseball cap, and off we went to watch our son play his first season of high school football. Dan had waited years to share that experience with his son, and I truly believe nothing, neither oxygen tanks nor pain, could have kept him from getting to the games. He died the day before the last game of the season, and the coach and players dedicated the game to Dan, noting he was *the* number one Parkway South Patriot fan. Even in his fading physical state, he didn't miss a play!

I WILL REMIND ALL THE FAMILIES I see in therapy to play. I will try to help them designate as much time for play as they do to stressing out and becoming hassled by the issues of daily living. Playing brings out the warm, pain-free parts of our characters. Our children and all those who love us need memories of those characteristics so much more than of what has been accomplished. Good times will be remembered. Why don't we play more? When passage to another world strips away the warm presence of a family member, it becomes crystal clear what the meaning of play is in life. Play leaves a legacy of laughter and love that cannot be diminished or stolen.

From the deepest, most desolate place within me comes a groan, a roar—please, oh please what I wouldn't give for one last chance to have fun with him again. If only I had known. I will remember to tell all families to please play while they can.

PEGGY NORTH–JONES works in the St. Louis area where she is a family and marriage therapist and an educational consultant. She has a daughter in college and a son in high school.

Joke Macabre

SUNDAY MORNING. JANUARY. I turn on the last act of *Der Rosenkavalier,* its fin de siècle Viennese waltzes winding around my little kitchen, dining room, hallway, living room, and back to the kitchen filled with winter sun. I'm going to make bread, but the cookbook releases a card with one of Al's recipes—à la alfredo. The bittersweet music sweeps through me. *Did you do it on purpose? The waltz inquires.* How often you made me Sunday breakfast after we attended the Saturday-night symphony concert. We would listen to the good-music station and argue the merits of Mozart versus Bach and so forth. Sundays still remind me of Al and our long-going platonic relationship. And I must admit that being recently divorced—after years of waiting on my husband—it was lovely to have someone make breakfast for *me.*

Al was contrary. If I had liked the soloist, he wouldn't. Al was supposed to take Coumadin, a blood thinner, but it made him feel more contrary. I'd warn him to take it, but he had a Teutonic mind: once made—forever adamant. Being a recovering dependent, I suppose I enjoyed butting heads with him, showing a growing ability to maintain my own opinion despite the fact that almost invariably Al got in the last word.

Al never laughed at my jokes. He had no sense of humor, yet, he loved beautiful things, and his house was a jewel. Besides CDs, he collected surrealist paintings, Picasso etchings, and dark, cloudy Ansel Adams photographs. I suppose, in a way, his love of luxurious surroundings was helping me to heal from my divorce, and so it was always hard to leave. Nonetheless, on Sunday afternoons I would drive my rental car to the airport and go back to my new job in Washington, and my status as 'single, head of household'.

I turn the oven on to 350 and enjoy Al's unique language on the recipe card while I wait.

Opposite:
Pierre Auguste Renoir.
Dance at Bougival.
Oil on canvas,
$38^{5}/8 \times 71^{5}/8$ inches,
1883. Museum of Fine
Arts, Boston. Gift of
Picture Fund (37.375).

The following recipe has been evolved by me and has been enjoyed by so many of my friends and neighbors that I've at last decided it would be simple laziness not to try and put its method in writing. With the exception of the final sauce, this dish can be made a day or two before it is to be served and the mixture stored in a common container in the icebox. This is of considerable advantage to the cook.

THE LAST TIME I VISITED AL we didn't have time for the customary leisurely breakfast because he was having company for Sunday dinner at noon with roast lamb and mint sauce. Al didn't like the way I set the table or made the lamb gravy. We'd had martinis instead of breakfast, and he began to get ugly. We usually had fun cooking together, so I held my tongue and, just as the guests arrived, offered to clear the table later between courses. "You might as well," Al sneered and pointed out the grease spots on my sleeve. "Of course there're spatters," I said with my newly emerging independence, "I made the gravy." Then I went obediently to the guest bathroom, rubbed my sleeve with shampoo and a face cloth, and joined everyone in the living room. The guests were the neighbors, with their out-of-town aunt (the guest of honor), and college-age son, Mark. The conversation went well. The salad Al had made was delicious, and the roast lamb was perfect. Al had put me at the end of the table, opposite his own place. "These people," I thought to myself, "probably believe we're going to become engaged." Even though we'd finished up the wine, Al said he wanted to make a toast. I quickly rose to clear the table starting with the glasses.

"*Don't you dare* put those glasses in the dishwasher," Al said. "I just bought them." I said the dishwasher would get off the finger marks. Ignoring his remark that any fool could get off the finger marks in the sink, I put the glasses on a tray.

"Dammit! Leave them on the table!" he yelled, grabbing the tray. The glasses swept off, and the beautiful prisms of chartreuse, amethyst, and gold rose through the air—like one of Al's surrealist paintings—onto the terrazzo floor in a tinkling heap. The four guests were ash-faced. "You clumsy woman!!". . . My heart turned to stone. Paternalism was something I had consciously cleaned out of my life. I knew I would never go back to visit Al again.

He called about the January concert—I said I couldn't come. He called in a few weeks and asked about a February concert. I said I couldn't come. He called a few days later to plan his fiftieth birthday party at the end of May. I said, "I might as well tell you Al—after the way you yelled at me—I made up my mind *never* to be available for your verbal abuse. *Never again. I'm not coming for your birthday!*"

HE NEVER HAD THE PARTY. At first he was threatening, then he clammed shut and didn't phone me anymore. Finally, in May, about the time of his birthday, he sent me a three-year calendar. I figured he would continue to try to get back at me, so I called to make peace and to thank him for the weird calendar. After that we continued a lukewarm telephone dialogue all summer and fall. I began to relent.

I've never been able to stay mad very long. I remembered how kind Al had been to me as I was recovering from my divorce. I thought of all the concerts. I thought about the breakfasts he'd made. In November, I decided to invite him to come to D.C. the next weekend for my own birthday. We had often celebrated it together, and he always remembered when it was coming up. He used to tease me with humorous presents tied up in lavender and old lace. Perhaps we could pick up from where we had left off. He might be an old-fashioned male, but we could be music-and-cooking companions again and let it go at that. But Al didn't answer my peace call. I phoned again on Monday and Tuesday. No answer. I called on Wednesday and let it ring twenty-one times. I called Thursday. Again a hollow ring. I knew Al wasn't there.

After my own birthday party, celebrated with my family, they told me. Mark had found him in his bed. Al had been dead for some time. The house smelled awful, Mark said.

YET, ALL OF THAT IS ALMOST FORGOTTEN on this winter morning in Washington with the dance music swirling around. Like the Marchallin, who in *Der Rosenkavalier*'s final act accepts her change to middle age, I recognize that I am left without Al's friendship and am now, truly, independent.

I wish I could phone Al in heaven and invite him to visit. We'd bake this bread together, argue about how much yeast, how hot the water. I slip the recipe card back into *The Joy of Cooking* and feel the beat of the bittersweet waltz. Those sweeping, sad crescendos will always remind me of Al. The music dies down and trails off at the end of the act. . . . I wonder how he arranged it. And with such perfect timing.

CAROL S. LAWSON is editor of the Chrysalis Reader series.

PATTE LEVAN

Follow the Man on Las Palmas

LAS PALMAS WAS A CROOKED, MEANDERING STREET, full of old tree-shadowed gardens and well-kept secrets and cats peering out of dusty windows from their hidden perches. It became the regular route for Jenny and me. We always discovered something new and mysterious we hadn't seen the week before.

Jenny was two years younger than I; her thick brown braids and large mouth dominated the small face, giving her a monkey look. She had just turned eight when she came to live with Cora, her maiden great-aunt, in the large, Spanish-style duplex across the street on Holly Drive. She was as good as orphaned, with her mother dead, her father in the Army, and her older half-sister in Villa Cabrini, a Catholic boarding school deep in the Burbank hills.

Prior to Jenny's arrival, the Burdett household had consisted of the two elderly sisters, Teddy and Cora, and Teddy's unmarried children, Hank and Lily, who chauffeured the sisters to their twice-weekly morning errands in downtown Hollywood, and to church on Sundays. They would emerge around 10 AM, a slow descent down the terra cotta steps and out the black wrought iron gate. Teddy looking imperious but fragile in an ankle-length black coat, her wispy top-knot held more or less in place by a small black hat and many pins. Cora hatless, in a print dress and long beige cardigan. Lily in slacks and camel hair overcoat dotted with cigarette burns. As the ladies carefully planted themselves in the back seat of the blue Ford, Lily would grin over at me straddling the large Sycamore branch that was one of my spy posts. She usually added a comradely wave as she drove off. The wave was eloquent; it seemed to express the absurdity of her life. I felt flattered to be included in this conspiracy; she assumed I

Joan Miró. *Untitled.* Oil on canvas, 38½×76⅝ inches, 1953. Cambridge: The Harvard University Art Museums. The Fogg Art Museum. Gift of Mr. and Mrs. Joseph Pulitzer Jr. (1972.361). New York / ADAGP, Paris: Artists Rights Society (ARS), 1996.

shared an understanding of the human condition beyond my years. When Hank drove, they took the green Packard. He would make the gesture of tipping his homburg and bowing in my direction. "Wa-al, good morning," he'd say, feigning delighted surprise each time at discovering me there. He never actually removed the hat; he was balding and wore it everywhere.

I had only been inside the house once, when I'd gone with my mother to return a book to Lily. Teddy had called me in to the dark, musty smelling kitchen and offered me some gummy green candy that looked as though it might have been in the cupboard since the house had been built. She said I could call her Theodosia. "Miss Teddy does prefer her formal name," Lily interjected. "Theodosia Burdett. A published poet, you know. In fact the poet laureate of Indiana. But it is a mouthful, isn't it?" She cleared her throat, indicating I was to respectfully take it all with a grain of salt. For some years, Teddy had been compiling a second book of poetry that she couldn't seem to complete; she would often lose a poem she was working on and accuse the family of stealing it to keep her work from being published.

Jenny and I both had missing fathers. Mine had left when I was six, and my grandmother had come to live with us until her drinking got so bad that my mother told her she had to leave. Terrifying as Grandma Grace could be, I missed her marching through the house at seven in the morning reading aloud entire texts of the latest murder trials in the old *Los Angeles Examiner*. I was as well-versed in the black Dahlia case and Chinese Mafia ring as I was in my multiplication tables. Then there was the year of the stepfather, a humorless man who disliked Gershwin and kept his suitcases under the bed in preparation for a hasty exit which was finally accomplished, to the relief of us all.

My mother worked long hours, and I read too much. With the arrival of Jenny, I was invited over to the Burdett house to play. I was the only child in the neighborhood. Jenny sat on the edge of Aunt Cora's bed, thin, pale, and nervous, her nose twitching. But there was a sparkle in her eyes, and I sensed that she would make a perfect compatriot under my tutelage.

Cora regarded me with a kindly but level look and invited me to Sunday School the next morning at the big Methodist church in Hollywood—a veiled command. If I was going to spend time there and become a suitable companion for her new charge, a price would be exacted. So Jenny and I went every Sunday and memorized the shortest Bible verses we could find, fighting good-naturedly over who got "Jesus wept" that first week. I showed her how we could palm one of our dimes, while dropping the other one into the collection plate. We kept back only one dime, deciding each week before we left who would be "it." I felt it wasn't honorable to withhold both of them. Afterward, we had permission to walk home as long as we went directly back to Holly Drive. We bought a forbidden candy bar with the purloined dime, and took the longest route, over Las Palmas Avenue, so that we could spot and follow suspicious looking people who might be saboteurs.

"What's a saboteur?" Jenny whispered nervously that first Sunday as we hit the street.

"They're spies," I said, pausing and staring at her to let the full weight of the revelation sink in. "But they're disguised to look like ordinary people. Don't you know that we're at war? We're surrounded by the enemy, so we have to be very careful." I was enthralled by talk of enemy subs sighted off the coast and the "Loose Lips Sink Ships" posters. I was hazy about what saboteurs did, exactly, but the word was irresistible, and we worked it into our whispered conversations as often as possible, speculating about this or that hapless person who came under our scrutiny.

It was several years into World War II, and the area surrounding the Hollywood Dam had been declared off-limits to all but military personnel to protect the city's water supply from possible saboteur activity. On hearing that, we put together a plan to hike up the side of the mountain, bypassing the road, and spy on whatever activities were going on at the dam. On the designated Sunday afternoon, I had the foresight to bring a small bottle of water, but the sun was hot, and the climb was steeper than we'd envisioned. We were scratched up and filthy by the time we reached the bank overlooking the dam, and the sweat was running in our eyes. There was no sign of a human being anywhere, just blue sky, water, and the scent of laurel bushes and dust. I realized Jenny was too tired to go back the way we had come without the possibility of a serious fall. We would have to take the road. To do that we had to walk part way around the dam to where the road began its curved descent. We had reached the gate and were slipping through the bars when a man in uniform started running toward us from the other side of the dam. "You kids get out of here!" he shouted.

"Keep running as fast as you can," I urged Jenny as we scrambled down the path, "he's going to shoot us. I'm sure he's not really a guard, he's a saboteur in disguise. But if he is a guard, we'll be put in jail."

We managed to ease unnoticed into the Burdett's downstairs bathroom and get reasonably presentable before supper. Jenny's face was a little paler than usual as we took our seats at the big mahogany table; other than that we looked like ordinary children returning from a day of normal play. Our replies to routine questions as to how we'd spent our afternoon were understandably vague. The knowledge that we were either going to be hunted down and killed because of what we knew, or arrested and jailed for trespassing, kept us living deliciously on the edge all that summer. We had, we convinced ourselves, encountered a real saboteur, and that was all that mattered. We told no one what had happened, not even Lily, who had become something of a confidant.

Sunday dinner at the Burdett's was always more of an occasion if Hank was in town. Hank was of course counted as one of our suspects, because he disappeared for days at a time when nobody seemed to know where he was, or to be the least bit concerned. But it was a stretch even for our fertile imaginations to picture Hank, with his baby face and affable smile, as a saboteur. Hank had been married at one time, had a now-and-then job selling advertising, and played dinner music at some expensive restaurant in town. Other than that, he was just Hank, and we knew nothing about him.

The big living room with its floor-to-ceiling windows was the sunniest place in their house. We sat reading in the late afternoon light, or pasting pictures from magazines into our scrapbooks, pleasantly exhausted from our detective labors, surrounded by the smell of Cora's pot roast or baking chicken. My mother would be over later with a salad, or special baked beans that Lily was fond of, when Lily could be coaxed to eat. Hank would finish his crossword puzzle and sit down at the old Gulbransen upright, his homburg at an angle, an unlit cigarette between his lips, the image rakish and thirties. He invariably started with *Honeysuckle Rose,* rolling into a fast stride bass that segued into *I'm Just Wild About Harry, Up a Lazy River,* some Duke Ellington. A long sip of his Scotch and water that had sprouted at five o'clock on the side table by the piano, then "What'll it be, ladies? I'm taking requests!" Lily or I would call out a favorite. "Wa-al, yes," he'd grin and bobble the cigarette between his teeth, "we can't leave that one out, can we?" He could play anything, and hunched over the keyboard, he looked like the happiest man alive. "Come on up here and sit with me and sing," he'd invite us. Jenny wouldn't budge. Some instinct prompted me to sit on the piano bench with him only when my mother was there, otherwise I stood looking over his shoulder at the sheet music when I didn't know the words.

Lily would hoot and wave her arms after each number, "Amen, brother," she'd shout. "Mercy!" She was seldom out of her chair except to refill her glass. "I'll eat later," she'd say. But she never did. Lily, my mother, and I often had lively conversations about books we'd read—until around 9 PM when Lily usually became incoherent.

"She's so brilliant," my mother said, "what a waste. If Lily had to get up and go to a job every morning, it would be a different story." My mother seemed to think the work ethic could cure everything.

One night when I was sleeping over, Jenny and I sat huddled in the dark stairwell giggling and triumphant after getting through our first piano recital. I had worn a hand-me-down dress that was too small, and it had split up the side, but other than that we had performed *The Jolly Farmer* and *The Young Prince and the Young Princess* without mishap. I asked her why she didn't play a duet after dinner with Hank when he asked her. "I didn't want to sit next to him," she said. "Whatever you do, don't sit on his lap." She told me he had put his hand up her dress and rubbed her leg once. She had run out of the living room and kept her distance from him ever since.

"Did you tell Aunt Cora?"

"NO!" she said emphatically. "I just don't ever sit on his lap, that's all."

His music didn't sound the same after that.

Jenny's father returned from overseas but, since he wasn't married, it was decided Jenny was better off with Cora until he could provide a proper home. A retired schoolteacher, Aunt Cora had imposed the structure she was comfortable with, with an emphasis on a well-rounded education, and Jenny had blossomed. Her twitch had disappeared, and she had grown sturdy. We daily concocted our own reality and invested ourselves in it fully; if we laughed hard enough at the adult world ours would triumph. We giggled our way through writing "I must mind," five hundred times when we broke Aunt Cora's rules, using our time out to perfect our imitation of Hank smacking his lips at dinner, or to shake our heads in the palsied way Teddy did when she couldn't locate a poem. Our mimicry of the sisters bickering over their finances was such a perfection of timing and dialogue that we became bold and performed it one afternoon for Lily, who snorted and hooted appreciatively, "Ain't it the truth, amen, sister!"

Lily often made the comment that her day had been exhausting. We knew that she had not moved from her chair, but we also knew intuitively that she had been working hard at something in her mind that was known only to her. We respected what she said, and we respected her, I think because she respected us. She looked us right in the eye when we were telling her about our day, squinting and nodding. It was a look that assured us that our thoughts were not only important, but perhaps profound. We never made fun of Lily. She was a fragile bridge between "our" world and "theirs." Lily's life before Holly Drive was sketchy: college, an executive position in an upscale department store, never married, an attempt at a relationship that had ended disastrously. She became a recluse in her late thirties. I learned all this as I came to know her in my high-school years. But at the time, the adults were simply our captors and caretakers. The rare ones who listened and could be trusted were our sounding boards. Their lives apart from that had no reality for us. By the time we were curious about them, they had left us, and the answers had to come out of our own lives.

Once a year in August, Lily deposited Aunt Cora, Jenny and me, and Cora's two grouchy cats at the Burdett's cabin in the San Bernardino mountains for three weeks. (Teddy had written a good deal of poetry about the wonders of nature, but she seemed to prefer to do it in Hollywood.) We swam, got sunburned, drank hot chocolate, played rummy, and slept outside. Jenny's older sister Irene often joined us for a week. That week we would move our sleeping bags further away from the cabin so that she could have a cigarette and say her rosary undetected. Irene smoked and prayed and held us spellbound every night with gripping tales of the hardships at Villa Cabrini and the cruelty of some of the nuns. She converted to Catholicism just before her graduation. Cora collapsed on the bed frequently with an ice pack on her head. Her energy was flagging. We giggled at her pointed black shoes turned out on the bed. She looked like the Wicked Witch of the West who had melted. We hadn't a clue that she truly loved us.

During the last year Jenny and I were together, the grownups held more and more conversations behind closed doors, and we eavesdropped. The sisters and Hank talked about Lily. She never ate, got dressed, or went out at all anymore. Scotch was delivered by the case from the liquor store, and she paid the delivery man extra to pull the empty bottles from under her bed and take them away.

The sisters and Lily talked about Hank. His "episodes" were becoming more frequent. We strained to hear more, but their voices had dropped inaudibly. We were frightened that they might know what we knew about Hank, as though somehow it was our fault.

I was thirteen and Jenny eleven when we learned that the episodes they had been referring to were bouts of depression, days and weeks when he was committed to a private mental hospital. This explained his mysterious absences that we remembered. And we learned that he had, at one time or another, half-heartedly fondled several young cousins and nieces in the family, including Jenny's older sister. Of course, nothing was done.

When Jenny was nearly thirteen, she was sent to live with her father and his new wife. She didn't want to go, but Aunt Cora felt she was getting too old to deal with a modern teenager. I saw Jenny only once more before she moved to Texas. The meeting was awkward.

She was immersed in a new life, and though we promised to keep in touch, I think we both somehow knew that we wouldn't. I was seventeen when Lily died. She was forty-nine. Cora said she'd talked about attending an AA meeting, but had never gone. Hank had his last episode when he took off most of his clothes and sat crying in the middle of Holly Drive. He was taken back to the hospital and died there a year later. Teddy lived to eighty-two, her second book of poems never published. Cora took her cats and went to live with a niece who was a photographer for *The Los Angeles Times*.

I became close friends with Jenny's sister Irene after she graduated from nursing school. We were talking about our families over coffee late one night. "I know your mother died young," I said, "but I never knew what she died of, was it cancer?"

Irene looked baffled. "Jenny didn't tell you?"

"No," I said, "we never talked about her mother at all."

"Our mother committed suicide." Irene spoke slowly. "She hanged herself with her nylon stocking, in the same hospital where Hank died. I can't believe you kids were best friends for all those years and she never told you."

"Maybe she didn't know," I said.

"Sometimes I think you're living in another world," Irene said.

I thought back to the five years of laughter, silliness, imagination, and joy that had marked Jenny's and my days together—another world. I felt chastised and foolish when Irene had said that. I don't feel that way now.

PATTE LEVAN, editor of the Swedenborgian news magazine *The Messenger*, holds a bachelor of arts degree from Antioch University. She is the author of a number of published works, including two novels, a nonfiction history of Parents Anonymous, and several booklets for the National Committee for Prevention of Child Abuse.

KEVIN D. BROWN

The End Zone

CAPTAIN TIMOTHY DIAL LIES IN THE CREASE formed by an adobe hut and the Baghdad street. He clears his mind and presses his long, thin nose into the dust. Suffering from oxygen debt, his powerful muscles quiver. The camouflage make-up he wears hides the features of his face: the serious brow, square and creased; the dark chocolate eyes; the shallow cheeks; and the thick, determined lips. He lies in the crease and concentrates on becoming invisible.

Cap'n Dial, your mission is only to identify the Iraqi communications center and report its coordinates scrolls through the active brain. Accomplished. He deletes these words from his mind and reflects on the fact that his classification has since been modified to disposable. The heavy, sweat-soaked fatigues he wears lack any identifying names or insignias. Men with families did not receive assignments like Dial's. Still, he did not feel alone. He had chosen his path in life. Yet from the moment his classification had changed, he had been gripped by an overwhelming desire to return home.

THE ANNOUNCER'S VOICE BOOMED from the press box on a cool October evening in southwest Iowa. A nervous Timmy Dial shook his arms and legs to keep them loose. He moved among his teammates—strapping deliberate farm boys and small darting neighborhood dwellers better suited to the more skillful game of baseball than the brutal sport of football.

At tailback, number 41, Tim - e - e - e - e DIAL! echoed, and Timmy charged from the sideline pumping his fist into the air. He leaped into the arms of his teammates and reveled in their encouragement as they vigorously pounded the sides of his helmet.

The red, white, and blue flag snapped in the autumn air as the small marching band struggled through *The Star Spangled Banner*.

Opposite:
Rufino Tamayo. *Man.* Vinyl with pigment on panel, 126×216 inches, 1953. Dallas Museum of Art. Dallas Art Association commission. Neiman–Marcus Company Exposition Funds (1953.22).

Timmy tried to swallow his nervous energy as he stared more intently than anyone else in the brimming athletic complex at the symbol of America. He was already formulating plans to serve that flag in the future, as his late father had done before him.

Timmy breathed the night air into his lungs, hoping the familiar aromas would settle the butterflies in his stomach.

THE EARTHY SMELL OF THE ADOBE wafts through the weary Captain's nostrils. He has not slept for two days, and he knows he may not get a chance to sleep for two more. For hours he has lain silent, muscles tense the entire time, like running a marathon in place. Concentrating on barely existing, he is a bug in the corner of the filthy street where it meets a barren adobe wall. The only reminder to him that he is alive is the irritation of the sweat trickling down the inflamed crevice between his buttocks, the result of perspiring heavily for five days without a bath.

Dial's location is a long way from the frigid temperatures in the mountains of northern Iraq where he was dropped from a low-flying military transport plane. He almost laughs aloud as he wishes his next mission to be in a location with more consistent weather conditions. Tropical islands like those in Hawaii and the Caribbean flash through his mind. Even in the Arctic he could better prepare his wardrobe. In the Iraqi mountains not even the heavy camouflaged material he sports keeps him warm. Now it is too much. He would love to shed his shirt, at the very least. But to leave traces of his presence could be fatal. Anything he removes must be carried, and he cannot afford an unnecessary burden. He must travel back to the mountains to be picked up.

Thick, exotic voices come down the street accompanied by softly pattering feet. Shop owners or street merchants, Dial thinks to himself. No immediate threat. He knows they cannot see him in the blackness of the night. He is merely a dark object, a street decoration to them. They would be upon him before they ever noticed he was a man, and then it would be too late for them.

Moments of strain pass. New footfalls approach; boots clump-clumping and stirring up dust on the Baghdad street. Eight sets of feet counted, policemen or possibly soldiers passing him. Still his heart rate and the tension in his muscles do not signal alarm. He is a phantom to every soldier on the streets of the earthen city. He knows they have merely sighted the bomber jets on their inadequate radar monitors, and they are scrambling to make a symbolic stand. Dial knows his time to lie in wait has passed. He must scramble, too.

TWIRLING END-OVER-END, the football arched high into the starry night, but Timmy Dial did not see it. He knew its destination and raced toward the smallish kickoff returner who stood anxiously awaiting the ball with his arms outstretched. Timmy barreled down the field kamikaze-like through the opposing players. Adrenaline coursed through his broad neck and chest. Like a lion ready to spring at the moment of attack, he was loose, saving all explosive energy for the moment of impact. He loved the air whistling through his helmet, the controlled insanity of playing on the kickoff team. A smile tugged at the corners of his mouth as he ran.

A whitish blur appeared to Timmy's immediate right. Abruptly, he was airborne, flying sideways. The turf, despite its cushion, came up fast and bruised his backside. In another situation Timmy might have relaxed and savored the comfort of the grass and the cool ground, but his embarrassment motivated him. He quickly rolled from his side to his back and caught a glimpse of a shadowy face inside a helmet turning away from him. The number 30 on the white jersey seemed to move slowly away from him as he wrestled with the waves in his brain. He jumped up and hurried unsteadily to the location where the kick returner had already been tackled. His cheeks burned red, but the butterflies were gone. He mentally prepared himself to make amends for his mistake.

THE POUNDING OF THE HEAVY BOMBS issues forth like the thumping of a big bass drum. The Captain moves from shadow to shadow in silence. He stops and, with an uncommonly accurate mental register, measures the clarity of the dull explosions in the distance. He tests the vibrations with his feet and makes a determination that can only come from experience in similar situations. He must move faster.

The sky begins to glow on the other side of the semi-barbaric city. Continual bursts of light, like stars shooting and falling, reveal the tall building tops in the near distance. As Dial stops for a moment, he peers upward from the darkness. He wipes some of the camouflage makeup from his eyes, the eyes of a shadow, constantly measuring, analyzing, considering. The impromptu light display makes Dial think for a moment what the heavens must have looked like when being created. Or, he thinks as a missile explodes just above the Baghdad rooftops and illuminates the smoke splattered sky, *a homecoming celebration.*

THE SMALL CIRCLES OF SWEAT that flowed out from the center of Timmy Dial's stomach and back now covered his entire mesh jersey.

His muscles burned, and the deep bruises covering his body had bruises on top of them. For three quarters he had carried the ball into the middle of the line. Huddled with his teammates, he chomped on his mouthpiece in frustration.

Timmy's mood grew somber as the fourth quarter began. Wide-eyed and expressionless, he abandoned any attempts at game time banter and focused all of his energies, mental and physical, on each play. Soon, bursts of adrenaline detonated periodically throughout his system, and he popped up from the turf with a renewed spring in his legs. He felt himself moving to a different level. It seemed to him as if the game had just started, and he was competing against those more tired and less capable than he. His plunges into the line gained more yardage. He snatched the football from the quarterback rather than waiting to receive it. He rushed back to the huddle time after time, ready for another try at the wall of defenders. The rhythm of Timmy Dial's heart pulsed through his legs, and his only desire was to keep that rhythm going. He knew this sudden physical mastery had nothing to do with his size, speed, or agility.

THE DARK FIGURE THAT IS CAPTAIN DIAL moves more carelessly. He does not linger in the shadows as before and openly runs from building corner to alleyway to any architectural indentation he can press his sweaty body into.

Wild-eyed citizens begin to fill the streets, hurrying over the dust that has risen and fallen in the same vicinity since the land was created. They do not notice the dark man that moves among them even when the explosions clearly light his sweat-streaked face. All they can see before their wide eyes is their own bodies crushed in the aged rubble if they do not flee.

Dial thinks about the invisible zone of safety that lies at the outer edge of the city. If compelled, he could stand with one foot on either side of that barrier. He is a master of precision, a paragon of the modern soldier. But he must focus on the objective at hand—running.

TIME TICKED OFF THE CLOCK. Timmy Dial was well into his second wind as he escaped the line of scrimmage, dodging, spinning, weaving for a first down. He now rose slowly from the tired mob of defenders it took to bring him down. Unblinking, he raised his head and strode deliberately back to the huddle. There was a tingling deep in his stomach that penetrated through to his spine. He glanced at the scoreboard. *Visitors 12, Raiders 7,* glared at him.

As the next play began, Timmy set his stance behind the quarterback. He knew the outcome of the game rested firmly in front of him. He envisioned it in his mind. The anticipation of celebration began to swell inside him. The quarterback barked the cadence, and Timmy reached for the conclusion he already pictured and grasped it as he grasped the final handoff. Battered by helmets and shoulder pads, his bruised forearms clamped around the ball to protect it during his final assault on the end zone.

THE CAPTAIN RUNS THROUGH THE EXPLOSIONS. Not just overhead now, but whistling and shooshing around him. His face is washed nearly clean by the sweat pouring down. He wipes droplets from his brow before they seep into his already stinging eyes.

Breathing is calm and steady as Dial's legs propel him through the calamity. The luxury of cover is lost. The frequently interrupted zig-zagging of his flight has become a more angular escape through the outer reaches of an erupting city. His energy is now provided by nerves and adrenaline. The escalating heat of the air around him prods him onward. A feeling gnaws at him as he moves. He wants to control the situation and attempts to do so with his running, but time grows short. The challenge becomes larger. And Dial thinks of a two-bedroom house with a deck he built himself where he grills bratwurst in the summertime.

The outer edge of the city, not far from the barrier of safety, comes into view and his speed increases. He pumps his arms, adding a few more crucial inches to each stride. Through his blurred vision his destination looks like *L'Arc de Triomphe*. In reality it is a simple shop, filled with incense, rugs, lamps, and the dreams of an owner who had hoped to market it as the gateway to the city. In the daytime, the owner congratulates himself for reaching customers on both sides of the street with his open-air displays and his divided store with its heavy wooden sign arching high into the air. The sign, its Arabic words carved deep into the wood, is the only structure joining the two separate halves. As explosions and their dancing lights begin to reach for the simple shop and its arching sign, the passageway resembles the entrance to a theme park in an old horror movie. Dial, appearing incandescent from the bursts around him, runs at the open space below the crude wooden sign.

HE RAN PAST THE LINE OF SCRIMMAGE. A hulking linebacker challenged him, but Timmy was already in full stride. He bent forward at the waist, lowering his head below the charging linebacker's torso. He raised up hard, driving his head and shoulders into the black and white of the opponent's uniform. Timmy did not lose a step as he ran through the linebacker, left clutching at air as he vaulted backwards.

With his sights already set on the goal post, Timmy Dial churned into the defensive secondary. The yards went by effortlessly. He broke to his right and ran for the sideline, the fast track to the end zone. His stomach was already celebrating. He could feel the spreading energy throughout the rest of his body. He could barely maintain the mental discipline necessary for him to run hard and smart.

Two smallish defensive backs came diving and grabbing for his ankles. His legs became rapid firing pistons as he forced his body between the two antagonists and ripped his feet away from them. He moved as only one solid muscle could move, the blood, the oxygen, the flesh, the force applied in unison toward one glorious objective.

The cheering hometown crowd rose as one. Because he was already in another zone himself, Timmy Dial did not hear the cheers, but he sensed the exultation as he listened to the breathing in his own head and felt the strength surge throughout his body.

Then his zone was invaded. A white blur to his left moved toward him. At the five-yard line the blur became a physical force as it dove and wrapped its strong arms around Timmy's striding knees. Timmy held every muscle in his body taut, resisting the collision as another body very similar in size to his own crashed against him. He drove his knees high and kicked out of the intruder's grip. The threat to his zone, his sanctuary, was successfully repelled. A dejected opponent, with a number 30 on his jersey, lay on the turf as Timmy Dial triumphantly crossed the goal line into the end zone.

THE CAPTAIN'S EARS RING FROM THE EXPLOSIONS close at hand as he presses toward the imaginary barrier of safety. He dodges to his right as a two-story adobe dwelling on his left instantly flares and transforms into a shambled one-story structure. A nearby shoosh-boom throws him to his left. He keeps his feet, but the subdivision of the simple shop to his right is gone. Its inventory of incense, rugs, lamps, and owner's dreams vaporized in a fraction of a second.

Dial sees refuge in the darkness on the other side of the now hanging wooden banner. Feet, then inches separate him from salvation. He feels a long forgotten tingling ignite in his breadbasket. He forces his uplifted right knee down into the ground and propels himself into a dive, driving his left knee upward at the same time for extra distance. He is immediately engulfed in silence and buoyed gently through the now brilliantly lighted air which penetrates even his tightly sealed eyelids. He knows he is traveling much farther than the strength of his own legs could possibly have vaulted him.

A barrage of questions burst upon his mind, though they are not new to a man who makes a living in the manner he does. Scraps of forgotten images flash over the movie screens on the inside of his eyelids. Every emotion he has ever felt passes through Dial's body in a microsecond. He is spent by this lifetime compacted and relegates himself to the invisible current carrying what he once considered as his Herculean body.

The benevolence of the powerful force does an about-face and cruelly reminds Dial he is still alive. His arms hang loosely at his sides as he is driven face first into the sand like a crash-landing airplane. The grimace of pain on his face allows the sand to push its way between his clenched teeth and into the pockets of his cheeks. He lies there for a moment, pressing his tongue against the cool granules. Then he raises his head, blows the sand out, and knows he must move on to get back home.

As Dial, now surrounded by the dark, lifts himself from the comfort of the earth, the ringing in his ears begins to subside, and he hears the rumbling of the artificial thunder already inflicting its wrath on another old neighborhood some distance away. The barrier held true, he thinks.

He begins walking, gingerly at first, then smoothly and rapidly, never once considering that his muscular legs will not be able to carry him home. Adjusting his eyes and his direction as he advances deeper into the blackness, he holds within himself something pulled from the flashes in his mind's eye only seconds before. It is the jubilation of crossing the goal line and entering the end zone. And though the necessity of his job has forced the Captain to quell his emotions, the feeling is more intense in him now than on the day he scored the dramatic winning touchdown in a game so many years ago. And the joy of going home after the game combines with the jubilation. The emotions grip him and permeate his being. But trailing behind is a slight sadness, for Captain Dial wishes he would have taken the time to relish the feelings when they occurred, rather than remember them under a rain of explosions a lifetime away.

KEVIN D. BROWN, who holds a master's degree in media communications, is a former English teacher now involved in program development for a nonprofit association.

THOMAS R. SMITH

The Blanket

I have thought so often about the happiness
we had during our first year together—
something about being in that small town,
something about being thirty-one.

We sang often because it pleased us,
pulled funny faces for the camera—
when we jumped on the blanket,
friends held the edges secure.

Over the years, the friends moved away—
or did we? There was no one to hold
the blanket. We still jumped,
but the landings got harder.

and sometimes we forgot to be friends
to each other. There was less singing,
the mandolin-top grew dusty, our
thirties were gone, and then—

Stories with only two people end sadly.
In our story there was a third who
dusted off the mandolin, called
back the village of friends

with a song: something about our faces
rising out of a pot of yellow tulips,
something about holding the edge of a
blanket, something about singing.

THOMAS R. SMITH's most recent book of poetry was published in 1994 by Holy Cow! Press. He lives in Minneapolis but says his inspiration derives from Wisconsin, his native state.

Bowling
on the Green

A BOOK ABOUT PLAY
ought to make you think about play in new ways,
understand it a little better,
and provide a measure of play's restorative
and creative power.
Writings to be read at play should be
fun to read.

Get comfortable, sit back, and have fun
with Part IV—
play in action,
play in print,
words that open gates in
inner fences
to let heart and mind play together.

PAUL HURLEY

The Cork Pops

Richard Haines.
Town Meeting.
Oil on canvas. 30×36
inches, 1952. Tempe:
Arizona State
University Art
Museum. Gift of Oliver
B. James. Photograph
by Ikuo Serisawa.

HEINRICH COULD NOT BELIEVE IT. The Wall had been there since the time he had been born!

But he could not deny the scene before his eyes. Something was in the air in East Berlin. So many people, all headed toward The Wall. Hundreds, maybe thousands, in the chill night air.

He found the celebrants an odd mix. Some people were solemn, some sad-faced and teary-eyed. Others seemed entirely unstrung in their jollity. He'd never seen anything like it.

THE WALL was only seven blocks away from where he stood. He thought he might go have a look. He wondered what the date was and had a feeling he would want to remember it. So he asked the man walking next to him.

"Oh, it's 9 November, Year of our Lord 1989." The man smiled. He shook his head lightly. "Can you believe it?" He jumped in the air, and his fist shot up as in the American car commercials. "I've always wanted to do that," he said. And then he began to cry.

Heinrich didn't know what to do. The man had changed moods three times in a matter of seconds. Most unusual. He looked at him again. They both stopped, two complete strangers, and held one another up as they proceeded to cry as they had not cried since they left their mother's cradles.

AFTER THE GREAT LIGHT that had been kept outside themselves entered their hearts, they looked closely at one another. "Heinrich Pfeffer," he said, offering his hand.

The other man, older, tall and grey-haired, with intense blue eyes, took the proffered hand and shook it firmly. "Karl Fischer. I'm pleased to meet you."

The night air was cool, but it did not matter. The two friends began to walk slowly toward The Wall. It was not a route familiar to either of them, for neither had been too fond of the sight of the thing. But they knew where it was, for all roads in East Berlin lead away from The Wall.

There wasn't much to say at first. "Do you really think it is coming down?" Heinrich asked. "It seems too good a rumor to be true."

Karl spoke with conviction. "The Russians are bankrupt, you know." He looked meaningfully at Heinrich. "It may even be too expensive for them to extort East Berlin."

Heinrich had a nice laugh at that; it tickled him. If there was one characteristic all East Berliners shared, it was a deep fondness for the irreconcilable.

An unexpected surprise came wheeling around the corner just then. A Russian army jeep drove by. The very sound of the jeep made Heinrich start in fear. It seemed to be in a hurry, but then who would not be?

He wondered what the crowd would make of the jeep, and he momentarily feared a nasty scene. There were thousands of East Berliners watching the jeep with its two uniformed occupants, nervously making its way through the crowds that wandered freely along the street.

The crowd, as one, faltered for a moment. The peculiarity of the situation must have stunned them. Nobody knew what to do. They all hung, a thousand listeners with the same question, for several long moments, at the crossroads of a great and painful confusion.

Luckily, the soldiers understood. They were prepared. They both had bottles of beer and the soldier in the passenger seat, an officer, stood up waving his beer. There was an insane joy on his face, and in his voice as well. *"Ich bin ein Berliner!"* he shouted in a dark and heavy accent. The look in his eyes was just manic enough to verify his sudden sentiment.

"He may be as much a victim of the times as any one of us," Heinrich said in a barely audible tone. It was the sort of thought he had not entertained before. The crowd seemed to agree. It laughed with one voice. A deep, hearty laugh that seemed to come from the ground beneath their feet.

The crowd waved them on. "Good luck to you," several voices said, "Keep out of trouble," and the jeep sped noisily on its way. Then the talking and laughter began again, a new and zany sparkle to it. "Somebody has popped the cork on Berlin," Karl said.

UP AHEAD, there was a brass band from one of the local schools. The musicians had set up on a street corner for no other purpose than to serenade the passing crowds. Somehow, at this late hour, they had managed to get into their uniforms and fall into step. Heinrich looked at his watch. It was nearly midnight.

Nonetheless, the music they made was perfect. Heinrich could hear them from a block away. He could not recognize the song, but he could tell they were perfectly in time with each other. Heinrich had always admired brass band music.

"It's Schubert, *Marche Militaire*," Karl said, divining Heinrich's thoughts. "I am an old trombone player myself," he added.

The two friends stopped when they came to the band. Nothing seemed more compelling at this moment than the music. It is a Berliners' sentiment, their deep love of music. "If The Wall is gone by the time we get there," Heinrich said with a puckish grin, "we won't miss it."

Karl's laugh came as a glow from an unaccustomed depth of heart. It was the greatest day of his entire life. He looked, clear-eyed, on a world of unexpected prospect.

The band had finished Schubert and was rewarded with applause and words of encouragement. It took a moment to tune itself. There was a hurried rustling of sheet music and then began another song. *"Edelweis,"* Karl said. "It was my mother's favorite." Absentmindedly, he started to cross himself, in old Catholic fashion. A burst of unreasoning fear upon him, he stopped short. He had not crossed himself in public for many years, and now suddenly there was no reason not to. The shock of compounded incongruities was too much; he began to cry again. Great, tearful sobs came wrenching free from the very heart of his heart. Heinrich looked on the older man with great sympathy. He had to hold Karl up for a few moments, once again. The man felt weak and limp in his arms. Several by-standers came and patted Karl on the back.

"There, there, my friend," one woman said. "We will see much of this before the night is through." With her hanky she wiped the tears from his face in a sacrament of sympathy and understanding.

Karl turned and looked at her. In his eyes was the wisdom of a confused joy and sadness. "It was my mother's favorite song," he said.

AFTER THAT, they began walking along with the faster pace of the crowd streaming toward The Wall. The mood of cautious reflection had left them. To have continued at their slower pace would have made them self-conscious, insubordinate to the enthusiasm of their neighbors. They allowed the flood tide of buoyant curiosity to pro-pel them along. An aura of expectant laughter filled the air.

They stopped once more, just a block or so from The Wall. There was a small delicatessen on the corner. The proprietor was outside laughing and talking to everyone who passed by, handing out free bottles of beer. "For the workers only," he shouted for all to hear. "This beer only goes into the bellies of those who will tear down the cursed Wall." The people around him laughed in approval. The gro-cery man continued, all smiles and joy. "Free beer for all those tear-ing down The Wall. Down the street they may have vodka for the oth-ers," he added. "But it is probably still for sale."

Both Karl and Heinrich took a bottle from the grocery man. They both got a hearty laugh from his antics. "The old Berlin," Karl said to his younger companion. "I remember the old one before the war," he said, his eyes looking within him now, trying to recall the sight. "I was born in nineteen and twenty-nine," he added softly.

The grocery man overheard and looked suddenly at Karl, as if he detected something in his voice. "They tore apart a happy neighbor-hood with that wretched wall, you know," the grocery man said. He and Karl exchanged a brief but deep look of recognition. Then he wiped away a tear and looked away to pass out more beer.

Heinrich continued his conversation with his older friend. "And I was born the same year as The Wall, in 1961," he said. "It is all I have ever known." His words hung in the air for several moments.

And then, as they negotiated a small bend in the street, The Wall suddenly appeared before them in its cold and unblinking banality. "I am a professor of political science at the university," he added.

Karl just nodded. "I see," he said, but his thoughts were already upon the pale monolith that appeared before them, garishly lit by a thousand spotlights. He looked, hoping to divine its secret. "I work in an electronics factory," his voice drifting away, hardly aware that he had spoken.

They stopped then, just a half-block from The Wall. The area in front of them had been cleared of all obstruction by the Russians years before—a killing zone. Off to the left was a wooden guard tower, tidy and recently painted, overlooking the scene. It was a smooth grey, bright, and unobtrusive. As recently as the day before, it had been manned by sharpshooting Russian soldiers. Today, two men with axes chopped at its thick wooden legs. One of the legs had been cut through, and while the tower listed slightly in the direction of its wounded member, the men began work on the support next to it.

"I know that man with the ax, the one with the red coat," Karl smiled. "He is a relative of my wife," his voice expressing a rich admiration. "I would not be surprised if he were the first one here."

The tower was now tilting drunkenly with each blow. The two axmen were cutting more carefully now, prepared to run from the tower's collapse. The crowd grew quiet, preparing to watch its fall from grace. There were then several thousands, watchful and expectant. A few voices shouted encouragement.

"Easy now," one man, a deep bass, offered.

"It is nearly done," another added.

"Free at last!" yet another voice intoned, as the axmen chopped through the second leg. But the tower was not yet ready to come down, though the axes had severed half its support. Merely it tilted forward somewhat more self-consciously. It prevailed on unexpected spine.

"German labor, German wood," someone offered.

Against the tower's hulking insolence, another man started a chain saw. He had been quietly admiring the work of the axmen, but now stepped forward to the whirling cough of his echoing machine. It was an oddly reassuring sound.

"It will be finished now," someone said. Heinrich recognized it as the clear baritone of the haberdasher from the street near the university. He caught the man's eyes, and they nodded silently.

The man with the chain saw finished his work on the third leg. He had carefully chosen the angle of his blade's approach. It had only taken him a half minute. And with that the tower came crashing down, the framework of its construction collapsing at its sullen contact with the ground. It seemed to heave a sigh of deep release. There were loud cheers that accompanied its noisy breakdown.

KARL TOOK A LONG DRAUGHT from his bottle of beer and set it down next to a lamp post. "Come professor. History is calling."

Heinrich obeyed happily. Soon they were among the busy, surprisingly ordered and considerate volunteers who were pulling at a section of The Wall. Heinrich guessed it to be about three and a half meters tall and two meters wide. One of the others turned to him. "It will be very heavy," he said. "When it begins to fall, get out of the way. I will shout to let you know." The large section of it—as thick as a loaf of bread is long—was nearly free.

A voice from amid the army of hands and hammers and pry-bars turned to the crowd and announced proudly for all to hear: "They are working from the other side. We can hear them!"

With that, the crowd gave out it loudest cheer. Heinrich recognized the sound of a cowbell rattling absurdly amid the glee. The cheer was answered immediately by a raucous volley from the other side.

A face, and then a second one, appeared above The Wall from the western side. *"Ich bin ein Berliner,"* the first of the young men said and waved a white handkerchief. He seemed more than merely pacified by drink, and Heinrich feared for the young man's balance as he made his way unsteadily to the top of The Wall. There he sat in pie-faced judgment. He was welcomed good-naturedly.

The second man was all anger. He was muttering to himself something barely coherent and apparently obscene about the Russians. He had a sturdy piece of wood with him, which he wedged into the opening created between the sections of The Wall. Never relenting in his tirade, he pulled for all he was worth on the piece of wood, trying to widen the crack in The Wall.

Soon they were joined by a lovely young blonde girl. Heinrich thought she was perhaps of university age. Her appearance was saluted by many whistles and much good-hearted encouragement. She had shapely, unstockinged legs that showed beneath her red silk skirt. From his post near the base of The Wall, Heinrich followed the legs fondly with his eyes, entirely seduced by their natural symmetry and wholesomeness. When he craned his neck a little higher so that he could look again at the girl's face, he found her smiling at him warmly, an artless look without a trace of self-consciousness. The simplicity of her cloudless blue eyes was expectant and focused.

The barelegged girl was joined by three of her friends, all musicians. There was among them a concertina, a guitar, and a pair of hand drums. As soon as they had made themselves comfortable on the top of The Wall, they began to play a lovely old dance tune. If anything, it reminded Heinrich of Paris, a city known to him only from the cinema. The girl began to dance atop The Wall, gracefully accommodating her steps and her enthusiasm to the limits of her precarious perch. She was an exceptional dancer, Heinrich reluctantly admitted. With her hands freely flinging the furls of her dress, she generously uncovered her legs for all those who watched the dance from below. It was a most elegant and poignant expression of the joyous expectation of the moment.

IN TRUTH Heinrich did little more than lean a warm hand against The Wall. It was a moral support more than anything, one that strangely filled him with a sense of worth. The seeming pointlessness of his existence was being drawn out of him through his hand. Suddenly he realized that he was a little tipsy from the beer. He looked up at the top of the loosened section of The Wall to see if it was moving. He could not be sure if it was. Incongruously, he had a mental picture of his mother at that moment, sadly telling a neighbor that it was her very son who had died when The Wall had dropped on him. Heinrich chuckled out loud and looked up again to admire the marvelous blue-eyed girl.

Karl, on the other hand, had grabbed one of the large pry-bars that had recently appeared and was struggling manfully, trying to free The Wall from its place. He, and many others in concert, made a great and violent exertion toward that end.

"Get out of the way," a voice shouted.

"Here it comes!"

And ever so slowly, pressed by long-separated neighbors from the other side, one section of The Wall came groaning down in Berlin. Once brought down, helpless and prone, it became the very bridge over which long-separated neighbors tearfully renewed acquaintances. Lying on its back, it became the vantage point of those who were leaving behind their old lives and beginning new ones.

There was much hugging, laughing, and crying; singing, praying, and dancing as old friends and new strangers embraced one another in that spot-lit space that had, but one day before, been the killing zone between the two halves of Berlin.

PAUL HURLEY is a California writer, musician, and composer.

LAURA L. TUCKER

Shepherdess of Play

I AM A SHEPHERDESS OF PLAY. I guide and protect young children in a family child-care setting. I have observed or participated in young children's play for many years, but it was not until recently that I understood my job as an early childhood educator with this new image of myself as a shepherdess of play.

For the past eleven years, each week I have transformed our one-hundred-year-old house into a place which invites, encourages, and supports play. Let me take you on a tour of my inside play spaces. I move a large low table into my spacious 1950s-style kitchen with its

Jean François Millet. *Newborn Lamb.* Pastel and black conté crayon on paper, 18½×15⅞ inches, ca. nineteenth century. Museum of Fine Arts, Boston. Gift of Quincy Adams Shaw through Quincy A. Shaw Jr. and Mrs. Marian Shaw Haughton (17.1513).

plantation of healthy greenery on the refrigerator top and faded linoleum floor. Here I set up messy, hands-on materials such as paint or clay. In the dining room, there is a low shelf with little figures and little houses that can be moved about to create various scenes in fantasy play. Up high, out-of-reach on my great-aunt's mahogany sideboard, curiously enough, I have my own childhood collection of china dogs, cats, and horses.

In the sunny living room, I place two trays on the floor with small manipulative materials such as puzzles, peg boards, or matching games. Children often play / work with these alone, and quietly. Often when I'm with my group of young children playing on the floor in this living-room space, I like to imagine that seventy years ago the same space was used for church suppers. This house was owned by the Ladies Aid Society of the Universalist Church across the street. I picture the women in their floor-length skirts busily serving their neighbors oyster stew at long tables set up in this very same room. At the other end of the room, I have a "Science Table." This is where we study objects from nature with magnifying glasses. Often the rocks or feathers from this table become part of a fantasy play. I might set up a seasonal tableaux with little figures or animals from natural objects for the children to move about in a story they create. Nearby are two child-size rocking chairs, each with a large teddy bear. These bears and chairs might be transformed into "Grandmothers in wheelchairs" or patients in a hospital, among many other possibilities. Also in the living room is an area that becomes either a firehouse with large fire trucks, a railroad roundhouse with large wooden trains, or a garage with large wagons. I rotate the various choices weekly. These vehicles encourage active and energetic play which is constantly moving from living room, to dining room, to kitchen.

And finally, the playroom might become a food co-op, a train station, a post office, or a campground. At other times, I leave the space less defined to allow the children more openness in the possibilities they create from their own imaginations. In the playroom, I have discovered that less is more, when it comes to toys. I have only the basic toys; building blocks, dress ups, little cars and trucks, little people, stuffed animals, and dolls.

Our tiny New England front hall is just big enough for the row of low hooks where hang the barrage of small-size snowsuits, jackets, mittens, galoshes, raincoats, scarves—the assortment varies according to Vermont's weather.

If I am truly a shepherdess of play, my job is not only to protect and guide, but also to give my flock of children the space, tools, and time in which to explore and discover their world. We spend a substantial amount of time outside every day, all seasons, rain or shine, balmy or blizzard. We do not watch television or movies. We do not play on computers. We do not play electronic games. I believe that through their play, children are learning and mastering necessary skills and finding their place in the world. They need to interact with their playmates, with me, and with the physical world, not with a machine or images on a screen. Only then will they be using all their senses to construct and reconstruct their relationships.

I have described the space and tools I provide the children in my care. What about time? Just as a flock of sheep need the green meadow in which to graze, children also need the time to be nurtured. My children are no different. They also need blocks of uninterrupted, unrushed time to play. And when given this time, with guidance, they learn how to share ideas with playmates. I have observed children finding out how to learn from one another. As one older child connects the large trains together, a younger child lies down on his belly and watches the peg attach with the next train. I have observed children become competent, confident, and caring in their relationships.

While children are playing, they are kinetically alive. Through their bodies, minds, and spirits they are connecting with one another like the train—with their imaginations, with their caregivers, and with the natural world. As a shepherdess of play, I have been given the honor to participate in a job which constantly reminds me, "I am alive!" What a gift my lambs give to me each day.

LAURA L. TUCKER lives and plays in Guilford, Vermont. In addition to operating her family child-care business, she currently teaches child development at Marlboro College and works with early childhood educators at the Community College of Vermont to help develop their skills as shepherds and shepherdesses of play.

MICHAEL ROBARTES

The Angelic Choir

Two Angels at the Nativity of Christ. Infancy of Christ window, Cathedral of Notre Dame, Clermont–Ferrand, France. Pot-metal glass, ca. 1190 to 1200 AD. Bryn Athyn: Glencairn Museum (03.SG.10). Photographer Leland A. Cook.

Surely their paths must have crossed. Although I have not come across any reference to an encounter between the Swedish philosopher Emanuel Swedenborg and the German composer Johann Sebastian Bach, it is likely that the two men did meet. In fall 1733, Swedenborg spent several months in Leipzig, seeing one of his publications through the presses of Friedrich Hekel. Leipzig was also the home of Bach, then cantor at the St. Thomas Church and at the height of his influence. St. Thomas was a Lutheran church, the same church that had been so much a part of Swedenborg's upbringing.

EMANUEL SWEDENBORG COULD HARDLY CONTAIN HIMSELF. Swirling eddies of sound rose up to the very sun! Spiritual light filled St. Thomas. Swedenborg shook his head in amazement. He tried to get a good look. This Johann Sebastian Bach—an energetic figure with formal wig, bobbing and weaving in and out of view as his hands played the immense church organ—knew something about music.

The power of an artist to transmute the deepest of human emotions with the ordered perfection of profound music was an endless fascination. Swedenborg knew he had to meet the musician. After the service, he quietly made his way to the back door through which the choristers and musicians had disappeared. As he entered through the door, his eyes searched right and left, but no one was there. Then, he heard a gaggle of laughing and commotion coming from a room down the corridor. Perhaps Bach was there.

Embracing and shaking hands all around, Bach *was* there, gratefully thanking all the musicians for the success of the service. The formal wig was off his head and sat on a shelf. Still young-looking, his face had not yet taken on the paunchy roundness of its later years. He was a large man, strong, with oversized, muscular hands. The air around him was afire with a bright enthusiasm. Bach looked up, and the two men momentarily shared a penetrating look. Bach reached out his hand. The gentlemanly Swedenborg reached out with his own, inquisitive at the thought of the power of the musician's grip. To his surprise, Bach's handshake was warm and soothing.

"Johann Sebastian Bach here," the robust musician said. "Organist, choir-master, and resident heretic of St. Thomas Church."

Swedenborg smiled. A happy, relaxed gentleman, this Bach. "Emanuel Swedenborg from Sweden. Scientist and writer."

"Oh yes," said Bach. "I have heard of you. A philosopher and man of God as well, is it not true?" Bach asked.

"Well, thank you," Swedenborg said, but not without a closer look. "I was not sure that my reputation had reached this corner of the Germanies. I would . . ."

They were interrupted by a lovely woman, younger than Bach, with a child at each hand. "Johann, the carriages are ready," she said. "If we do not go now, we will miss the dinner at cousin Witfels."

Bach shook his head. "This is Frau Bach," he said to Swedenborg. "Anna Magdelena."

Swedenborg bowed his head in her direction. "Madam," he said.

Abruptly Bach was in motion toward the door. "Excuse me, sir, I really must go." He stopped in the doorway to have another look at Swedenborg. "First a visit with the relatives, and then I go to play at a wedding." Something unfinished held itself in the air. "But won't you stop by tomorrow morning for some coffee? Our quarters are right here on the church grounds."

"Certainly," Swedenborg said. "Thank you for your kindness. I look forward to seeing you again."

Bach was gone.

SWEDENBORG WAS UP WITH THE SUN the next morning. The Leipzig air had a certain chill in early autumn. A lovely, well-ordered city it was, the early fall color just then coming into the tall ash and maple trees that lined the streets. Soon the birds would fill them with song. From the second-story window of his room he could see the stacks of new-mown hay around the countryside edging the city. The fragrance was earthy and somewhat penetrating.

He decided to walk to his appointment with the Leipzig master. Swedenborg often enjoyed the relaxing strolls that so harmonized his being with nature. After such a walk, life tended to take care of itself. And so, as the city of Leipzig awakened to a cheerful autumn day, Emanuel Swedenborg quietly strolled its tidy streets, his heart as light as the merry bird song coming from the trees above his head.

The clanging of the bell-tower, austere and precise, struck nine times when he arrived at Bach's residence. School was in session in a nearby building, and Swedenborg could sense the bright attention of the children as he strolled past the open windows of the classrooms.

Standing before Bach's door, he could hear the tingling of a harpsichord. He listened for a moment. Someone was playing two-handed scales at a furious pace. He waited at the door listening, not desiring to interrupt the man in his work. When there was a lull, he tapped the dull-sounding brass knocker.

It was Bach who answered. "Ah, Baron Swedenborg," he reached out his hand again, and Swedenborg took it. Those hands were an anomaly. The appearance of a working man's hands—a farmer or a laborer—but with such delicacy . . .

"So glad you could visit us again. Do you wish coffee?" Bach asked.

Swedenborg cleared his throat. His voice was a precise and resonant baritone, a man to be listened to. "Yes, of course," he said.

There were piles of manuscripts in one corner, the harpsichord in another. One wall was filled with books, while on another were hung several stringed instruments. Swedenborg walked toward the bookshelves. "I don't know if I told you that I play the organ myself and how much I enjoyed your music yesterday." He turned to look at Bach. The composer was all smiles.

"Thank you," he said. "The music," he paused thoughtfully, "often seems to write itself, you know."

Soon Frau Bach entered with coffee, her movements quick and decisive. Swedenborg gazed at her, an attractive woman, bright-eyed and alert. She looked perhaps ten or fifteen years younger than her husband. She wore a light blue dress of a flowered print, cut rather low at her abundant bosom. "Johann tells me you are a famous philosopher visiting us from Sweden," she said.

Swedenborg smiled. A charming lady, with a soft, soothing voice that put him entirely at ease. "I'm not sure that everyone would be so generous, but, well . . ." his face grinned, "yes, I guess I do rather abstract at times."

That brought a silly, incongruous giggle from all three of them. Swedenborg was beginning to feel right at home. Anna Magdelena, having placed a cup of steaming coffee before each of the men, was by this time at the door. She smiled at him warmly. "If there is anything else I can get for you, please call me," she said and left softly.

Swedenborg walked to the window. He warmed himself in the bright light of the sun. Outside, at the far end of the church grounds, one of the children's classes was having recreation hour. Their laughter filled the air.

THE CONVERSATION TURNED TO MUSIC. Swedenborg discerned how willing Bach was to discuss his music, and he directed their discussion toward it.

"Your reputation, Meister Bach, has preceded you," Swedenborg offered. "You are spoken of as one of the great keyboardists of Europe. I wonder if you might play something for me."

Bach nodded approvingly. "I was hoping you would ask." He was already in motion toward the harpsichord. "Is there anything in particular, my friend, you would like to hear?"

"Well, yes. I've heard you can improvise fugues, *extempore,* if you are merely given a melody to start from."

Bach was pleased. "Yes, it's true. There is a bit of the showman in me if you wish to know the truth." He looked at his new friend. Swedenborg peered somewhat quizzically back at him. "But all founded on learned musical principles, you can be sure," he added with a laugh.

Swedenborg smiled. "Of course."

Bach was back at his scales. His hands flew rapidly from one end of the keyboard to the other, accurately and squarely landing on each note. Bach raised his voice over the restless commotion. "There is perhaps a melody you know that might serve as a theme?"

Swedenborg thought for a moment. "There is a children's song I have heard several times in Paris. Perhaps you know it. It goes," and Swedenborg began to sing, *"Sur le pont d'Avignon . . ."*

Bach was right with him . . . *"mi-fa-sol-do, ti-do-re-sol."* He was already going over it on the harpsichord half in thought, half in conversation. "This is the one you had in mind?" he asked. Swedenborg nodded, and Bach played it through a second time, already harmonizing it with a bass line. "I have heard the children sing it many times myself," he said without looking up. "It will do just fine."

Soon he had it in two voices, the second one entering in the left hand, in a lower octave, at the distance of a fifth. A few moments later, it reappeared up much higher. Before long, Meister Bach had the melody going in four places at once, sounding as if the Lord himself had meant it to be played so. "Most impressive," Swedenborg said.

But that was only the beginning. Bach held his listener transfixed, racing up and down the keyboard, the melody in a multitude of settings and contexts. Swedenborg shook his head in amazement. When Bach finished with a long, theatrical trill and flourish, Swedenborg stood up clapping his hands. "Bravo, Maestro, bravo!"

The conversation took another turn. "Now, I've held center stage for much too long," Bach said. "If I'm not very careful, I will begin to bore you. Anna Magdelena is always saying that I get too absorbed in my work. You must tell me something of your work and what interests you most at this time?"

Swedenborg thought for a moment. He brightened. "I have been thinking of angels lately . . . the good and the bad of them," he said. "You can see, I'm not entirely the practical scientist."

"Quite the contrary," Bach said. "What could be more practical than speaking of God's blessed messengers? I think of them often myself."

Swedenborg gave his host a curious and surprised look. "I see." He continued after a few moments. "My chief concern is the need to extend scientific thought beyond the limits of mere materiality, mere function and convenience." He turned to look back at his new-found friend. Bach was listening intently and nodded in agreement as Swedenborg went on: "I've come to see the great problem of our age is the unwillingness of man to extend his imagination beyond the realms of the merely functional." He paused again. "Do you understand what I mean?"

"Yes, it's as if earth is earth, and heaven is heaven, and never the two shall meet," Bach added.

"Yes," Swedenborg nodded his head. "That's it." He walked back to his chair and picked up his coffee. It had by then become cold, but he nonetheless found it delicious. "More and more my work is going in this direction. I've come to see that material needs, when they are fulfilled in a man, often satisfy him to a point where he separates himself from God. That the fruit of man's labor in the present day is to create a stupor of self-satisfaction," he said with emphasis. "I often find it most frustrating." Now he began pacing the floor, intent on his thoughts. "Something must be done to rekindle mankind's desire to seek and serve the kingdom of God." He looked over at Bach. "Am I making any sense?"

Bach looked at him appreciatively. "Quite so." He smiled to convey his sympathy. "The pursuit of material comfort—the pursuit of much practical knowledge as well—has come to take the place of the inquiry to seek and know the kingdom of heaven, is it not true?"

"Yes," Swedenborg said. "That is well expressed. The pull of the senses, if I may, has come to dominate us."

Bach sipped his coffee. He looked up and offered with a good-natured recklessness, "Well, surely to be occasionally vanquished by the senses won't hurt a man." And he gave a big laugh. Their eyes met curiously. "I refer to the pleasures of married life," he said with an impish grin. "But I change the subject. Yes, we must all guard against that sort of spiritual lethargy. I agree—it is the great problem of the day." He brightened once again, rather suddenly. "Perhaps this will help. In my work, I find that music can inspire the mind in the direction of communication with spiritual forces." He paused for a moment to look at Swedenborg. "Our sensuality is not hopelessly opposed to our higher sense. One must understand the nature of beauty itself, my friend," Bach said with emphasis. Again he looked intently at Swedenborg, drawing out the man's intelligence. "We could say that beauty is the attractive quality of truth, could we not?"

"Yes," Swedenborg agreed, alive with the fire of his profound intellectual passion. "Well said. That is the message of the angels. It is what they say to me at all times. That God's order and truth is great and in perpetual manifestation about us." A pleased smile passed across his face. "The kingdom of heaven is here amongst us," his voice rose impressively, "and not in some distant abstraction."

Bach's eyes sparkled. "You might be surprised to hear the angels are this old musician's good friends as well." His voice also rose with conviction. "In truth, they are the very source of all inspiration, of whatever sort." He went to the harpsichord, eyes intent with an inward focus, playing rather softly a piece for four voices, moving calmly, majestically. Beautiful though it was, Swedenborg was not familiar with it. He was about to ask its name, when to his surprise Bach shushed him.

"Do you hear that?" Bach asked.

The air brightened greatly around the two of them. Swedenborg felt his heart fill to its very limit. His eyes became widened and tear-brimmed. Above and around them, the room filled with the pure tones of an angel choir, in full concord with one student who sat at the keyboard and another who stood at his side. The angels were lovingly intoning the four voices of Bach's Christmas hymn *Wie soll ich dich empfangen? [How Shall I Receive You?]*

MICHAEL ROBARTES is a California writer, who is currently writing the libretto for an opera.

ELIZABETH GUTFELDT

Grandmother's Secret Garden

Elizabeth Gutfeldt. *Untitled.* Collage, cut-out paper, 1996.

WHEN I WAS YOUNG, my favorite book was Frances Burnett's *The Secret Garden,* a story about the great healing power of a garden for two lonely children who were transformed through its power. Perhaps that book was a favorite in part because my grandmother was the first to read it to me, but also because of my own early experiences in her California garden.

The first three years of my life were spent in Berkeley, in a little house next to my grandparents'. Our back yard was nondescript, but behind it was a magical place, surrounded by high walls and fences, and filled with fruit trees and flowers. My grandmother's garden!

How I loved that garden! My grandmother would take me along when she was working there, and I could play on the winding paths or hunt for little berries to pop into my mouth. It was a wondrous place, full of glorious flowers glistening and sparkling in the sunlight. Beautiful bright orange butterflies flitted around the lantana bush, tempting me to toddle after them. And the sun shining through the fruit tree leaves blowing in the wind made light and dark patterns on the ground, which absolutely fascinated me. I remember eating bright currant berries that glowed like polished red glass beads, bursting open when bitten, releasing their juicy, sour goodness.

I can remember at other times my grandmother holding my hand and walking up and down the little paths in the garden helping me hunt for raspberries just for me. We would laugh and giggle and tell secrets at our tea parties with delicate hand-painted plates and cups and little slices of pound cake with jam on top.

Grandmother would let a bit of her inner child out, and we were like two little girls together. We imagined what it would be like to wake up in heaven, painting word scenes of beautiful places and loving people. The garden would seem full of angels; we would laugh and twirl around together. Sometimes we would pick flowers and ferns to make a beautiful bouquet for my grandparent's dining room table. They always had fresh flowers in their house.

There were vegetables in the garden, too. I was fascinated with the asparagus plants, so feathery and fern-like. It was hard to believe that they really had been asparagus, that if you let them grow, that's what they would come out looking like.

I remember one day specifically; someone had left the back gate open, so I toddled alone out into Grandmother's garden. I saw the beautiful flowers and wanted one. They were purple irises. Reaching out, I grabbed one, closing my little fist over it, squashing it. When I opened by fist, I discovered to my dismay that I didn't have a beautiful flower at all, I had a bunch of crushed petals. I remember my tremendous disappointment, then reached out and pulled another flower, and again squished it in my hand. I realized that it looked all torn and maimed and not pretty anymore.

I saw angel spirits many times in the garden. They were beautiful beings of light, with vibrating iridescent auras around them that looked almost like shimmering wings. I saw them among the trees and flowers and joyfully communicated with them. They told me that I was whole and needed to be treated gently like a flower, that God loved me no matter what I did, that I didn't have to be "good" to win love. It was a different concept of life. This was probably my first idea of God, apart from what I was taught. Of course I was too young to put it into words at the time I first experienced it.

It was always a delightful experience, the sense of being in grandmother's garden alone. It was a whole different world. No one else knew that I had special experiences in that garden—it was a precious secret I didn't share with anyone. That garden remained with me as a memory of a kind of life that was creative and affirming. I had memories of going into that garden where the light and dark shadows flickering over the delicate flowers were irresistible.

We moved far away after I turned three, and I missed my grandmother and her garden terribly. Those were the Great Depression years. Daddy was out of work, trying to make ends meet with odd jobs when he could find them. When life became particularly turbulent or confusing, or when I was hungry for a moment of joy, I would shut my eyes and fantasize back to that garden. It never failed to bring peace and comfort. I could remember the time back in Berkeley when my life had more meaning, when I was being heard and understood.

The spiritual experiences in the garden made the deepest impression on me, experiences that seemed more real than the outside world. Later on, when I would hear stories of good fairies, I would think of those early times. Even in Bible stories when an angel appeared or spoke, I would connect it with what I saw and felt and communed with in my grandmother's garden. There was a healing power between those walls, a focal point of unconditional love and understanding.

Each of us holds early memories of spiritual awareness within, though they may be fleeting, and not always available for conscious recall. These memories have the potential for forming a healing retreat, a respite from external trauma and frustrations, a sacred space for connection with the divine. There are many who have been aware of similar phenomena, but the most universal description of this I found in Emanuel Swedenborg's writings. He describes how every person who survives childhood has had moments in infancy or young childhood when they experience enveloping love, feel truly understood and accepted, or experience glimpses of truth of the divine. These childhood moments have tremendous healing power when they are remembered and re-experienced. Swedenborg referred to these memories as "remains" because they remain with us throughout our lives, at least in our subconscious, where they form a bridge between worlds. They are usually not brought to light unless we are in a state that can really honor and treasure them.

My early garden experiences have helped me as I daily prepare vegetables for my husband's special diet. Growing vegetables and pulling weeds, I am thankful for the nourishment of plants that have become allies for his battle with cancer. In my bittersweet moments of thanksgiving, my remembrances of the secret garden and my grandmother have given me the strength required to deal with these current nutritional needs. I am able to accept the reality that my husband's life on this earth could have been crushed several years ago—like that childhood iris—if it were not for the work of my caring hands in tending our garden.

ELIZABETH GUTFELDT holds a doctorate in psychology from the University of California. She lives in Berkeley, the city in which she grew up, dividing her time between playing flute in an orchestra, enjoying grandchildren, creating art in various media, and working in her own beloved garden.

SUSAN FLAGG POOLE

Timeless Keeping

SWINGING IN AN APPLE TREE, hanging upside-down, and getting dizzy with delight, I was in heaven. All senses were alive. Seeing the world around me, touching the rough bark, smelling and tasting the crisp apples, listening to the honking geese, feeling the gentle breeze wisp through my hair, the leaves shaking with the branches—all of this made me feel a joyful part of creation. Everything blended into one timeless moment . . .

Watching my children at play reminds me of that clockless time of wonder and makes me feel like a child again. My son Aaron stirs up the ocean water at night, creating flashes of light. To him, the bioluminescence from microscopic fauna is magic. Fascinated with the sparkles jumping over the water, he calls to his sister.

"Rachel, come see this. It's awesome."

Eddie Arning. *Nine Figures Climbing Trees.* Oil pastel and pencil on wove light green paper, 32×22 inches, 1972. New York: Museum of American Folk Art. Gift of Mr. and Mrs. Alexander Sackton (1985.01.10).

Enchanted, Rachel asks why are there stars in the water.

Aaron explains, "The creatures in the water are getting excited."

This flashing luminosity awakens feelings of awe and wonder. The children laugh, giggle, and ask questions. They want to know why the water sparkles. Their play creates a natural learning situation for understanding more about these microscopic creatures. I could see, feel, and hear the joy they experienced in their playful discoveries. Their excitement was contagious.

The innocence of children at play corresponds directly to their inner state, according to the eighteenth-century mystic Emanuel Swedenborg. Inner feelings are exhibited outwardly in smiles, laughter, and motion. When Rachel ice skates, she demonstrates this 'gladness of mind'. She glides along with ease, her arms sway gracefully, her face is peaceful and relaxed, her body moves effortlessly. Every part of her seems coordinated and rhythmic. She loses all sense of time and appears to be somewhere else. When it's time to go, she'll invariably say something like, "Oh, no. Already? But I just got here."

When I listen to music I myself lose all notion of time. I forget problems and relax. My friend Ingrid and I would play piano duets for hours when we were children. Totally engaged, becoming more animated with each piece, our fingers would fly across the keys. Landing on the last note simultaneously, we'd laugh uncontrollably, being so keyed up that sometimes we'd fall off the piano bench. Our relationship was deepened by the synchronicity of our experience.

At play, children really do feel swept away. When Rachel and her friend jump rope, the rhythm and repetition in their songs sound like sacred chanting. Unified in movement, responding to the heartbeat of play, jumping rope provides pleasure. When I asked Aaron and his friends why they like to play Kick-the-Can, they said it is so absorbing that they don't think of anything else when playing it. Aaron says he likes it when his adrenaline gets flowing and he becomes active, excited, and scared all at the same time. The delight, ecstasy, and fright of being caught in the dark changes the way he feels.

Transcendence occurs when we're alone, facing the unknown, the unpredictable—looking into darkness, not knowing what it hides. Going beyond oneself is a common childhood experience, we awaken at unexpected times with flashes of illumination. Brief insights into the mysteries of life (dark and light) can strike anytime, anyplace, anywhere. Fast and as unpredictable as lightning, the flash can leave an everlasting impression. These are moments that will live in our memories forever.

I remember experiencing these feelings when playing Hide-and-Seek as a child. This game was indeed a mystical experience. In the dark, hiding from my friends, I felt a presence all around me. I was scared and excited about suddenly being caught, but I also enjoyed being alone, totally absorbed in the dark moment.

Sharing the spirit of play leads to feelings of closeness and unity within a group. Quaker Meeting, one of our favorite games, took place in the confines of our ancient attic. My friends and I climbed up a long flight of gray painted steps, unlatched the door, and crawled under the eaves into a circular space lit up by two tower windows. We sat cross-legged in a circle on straw mats. With arms crossed, we stared at each other with dour expressions. Then someone banged a heavy gavel three times. We said in unison:

Quaker Meeting has begun.
No more laughing, no more fun.
If you show your teeth or tongue,
You will have to pay a forfeit.

We remained seated in our circle, solemn as possible, our lips, tightly closed, very, very serious until someone broke the silence with a burst of laughter that could be contained no longer. Then we said to the person who laughed:

Truth, dare, consequence, promise, or repeat!

If the loser chose "repeat," we made up a ludicrous task, such as "I will kiss Harry at the bus stop in front of the bus driver," or, if the victim chose "dare," we said, "We dare you to jump off the shed roof." Next we gathered at the shed roof, taunting and teasing until the victim jumped. We felt as if we all belonged and enjoyed the challenge given from some member of the group. Today Quaker worship is not just a game for me. I have experienced sacred moments waiting in silence. Quaker tradition values making decisions by consensus. Cooperation and sharing responsibility with a group gives life and energy to any activity.

In the summers, I often invited a friend to my house to play marbles. We dug a hole in the dirt, smoothed the surface around the hole, and admired the colorful designs of the glass marbles. I loved the challenge, the competition, the triumph of winning, and I practiced to perfect each movement. I developed the skill of effective shooting, but quickly discovered that, if I didn't give some of the marbles back to the loser, there would be no one to play with for the next game. "Playing for keeps" could prove counterproductive if the ultimate purpose was to have fun. We learned early on that giving and receiving was crucial if you wanted to keep the game going, and we could play all afternoon without noticing it was getting dark.

A cellist friend says that there are no words to describe the timeless experience of being a part of the symphony orchestra. Totally absorbed in the music as he "plays" the cello, he feels connected to others and to something greater than himself. With the music flowing in and out, keeping time with the other instruments, chronological time disappears. He feels transformed. Monks feel transformation as they chant in unison. Their individual voices actually produce more than one tone at a time. The deep tonal chords vibrate within, lifting them to incredible feelings of inner peace. When they chant together, their individual voices combine, transforming each chanter into a deeper state of consciousness.

When I was growing up, work was play for me (and still is). During apple-picking time, my family gathered at the orchard and began working. We dropped the luscious apples from the trees, filled our baskets to the brim, and later bounced them into the cider press and at each other. We chopped, squished, and pressed the apples until the sweet juice began to flow into the jugs. The cider was delicious, and so was the experience of working and playing together. When we were finished, we gave the cider to relatives, friends, and neighbors, and sold the rest in our country store. Autumn harvest always fills me with fruitful memories. Family ties like these go on from one generation to the next. Every time I taste an apple pie, I am thrown back in time, and the present moment disappears.

Childhood games, music, dance, powerful memories, the beauty of the earth, special friendships, all can evoke transcendent states of mind. Each is precious in its own right. Each conveys a divine energy. Each is timeless. Yet, each is fleeting and constantly changing.

As I open my eyes to what's happening right now, I see my children playing outside in a huge leaf pile—they are supposed to be raking up the leaves—and I am reminded that time and space don't exist in the interior world of play. As I become more aware of the value of including more play in my adult life, I am forever learning and struggling to balance external concerns with what really matters. Right now I think it's time to go outside and rake up some fun.

SUSAN FLAGG POOLE is a teacher, writer, development editor, and mother. She lives in Wilmington, Delaware, and Friendship, Maine.

KATE RANSOHOFF

The Black Pearl

THE VILLAGE OF BRAUGHN sits in rolling hills, amidst fir trees, a rushing river, and pasture lands, with a school, an inn, and a meetinghouse by the common. Long ago, a most unusual Peddler arrived. The village welcomed him. And thus, he stayed many years at the inn, talked with elders, tended animals, and told stories. The Villagers grew robust, laughing and singing. Fewer squabbles and disagreements arose. One dawn he left without a word, leaving a Black Pearl nestled in a soft leather bag on the desk of the Inn. An iridescent glow emanated from the Pearl. The Villagers, saddened by the absence of the Peddler, remembered his tales and told them to each other, to the young, and to visitors. They build a special cabinet for the Pearl so that anyone who wished might come to see it. But, unhappily, one night the Pearl disappears—almost as though it has been wafted away by magic.

SOMETIME LATER, THE ANGEL URIEL delivers a message to Winslow, the flying Dragon. On the earth directly below, the Elders of Braughn discuss the steady decline of their village. They have come to realize that this decline is somehow connected to the absence of the Peddler and the unexplained loss of their Black Pearl. They decide their best hope for returning vitality to Braughn is to recover the lost Pearl. They select a youth, Haddad, to make the trek to find the Pearl and to bring it back. At this exact moment, the Annual Gathering of Birds is convening in the branches of the Big Tree on the shores of Lost Lake.

THE ANGEL URIEL AND WINSLOW THE DRAGON, land on a wind-tossed cloud to talk. The cloud immediately pours rain onto the land below. Thus, the two remain hidden from the eyes of humans. Uriel tells Winslow, who has a passion for daring adventures, that his newest assignment is to watch over Haddad. He enlists the support of the Birds in bringing laughter back to the youth. When found, the Pearl is to be placed in Winslow's belly-pouch until the day arrives when the Pearl is ready to be given back to the village. Uriel assures Winslow he will know when that moment has arrived, then the dragon's job will be completed. Winslow thanks Uriel for the message. They embrace and part.

WINSLOW HURRIES TO THE STONE where Haddad is resting and sits down. Haddad, weary, lonely, and worried, is so relieved by the appearance of someone to talk with that, without introduction, he pours out the sad tale of Braughn. Ever since that shocking morning when the Pearl was discovered missing, people had begun to argue, fight, and threaten each other. Gone was the Braughn that was calm, orderly and friendly. Fear and jealousies grew and grew. Haddad was here seeking on behalf of the village to bring the Pearl home.

WINSLOW TAKES HADDAD TO THE BIG TREE WHERE THE BIRDS ARE GATHERING. One by one the birds introduce themselves. Winslow says, "Each bird is beautiful in a particular way—in each uniqueness lives a special talent—the deep mouth of the Pelican, the long legs of the Flamingo, the raspy squawk of the Parrot, the round eyes of the Owl, the Peacock's . . ."

"Gorgeous tail!" interrupts Haddad as a wide smile erases his worry and he laughs a full-throated laugh. The Birds, joined by Winslow and Haddad, dance, sing, and tell stories until bedtime.

EVERY DAY AT DAWN HADDAD SEARCHES FOR THE BLACK PEARL along the water's edge, and at noon Haddad swims in the lake and looks below the lilypads, in the crevices of rock, and among the pebbles at the bottom. At sunset, Winslow prepares a meal and, in the company of the Birds, they share stories. In the cool dark of the night they lie on the ground, and Winslow folds his wings about Haddad as a blanket. The Birds watch over them both so that no evil spirit or scary dreams break into their sleep. One noon Uriel, invisible, drops the Pearl into Haddad's palm. Haddad returns to the Big Tree bursting with song. With great gusto and joy a feast is prepared.

PLANNING BEGINS FOR THE RETURN TO BRAUGHN. Winslow offers to tuck the Black Pearl in his belly-pouch to keep it safe on the trip, and Haddad hands it carefully to Winslow. The Birds offer to be their scouts and protectors. Harvest is near in Braughn. The Villagers, busy gathering and saving for the winter, are short-tempered. Irritation is common. Early one morning Winslow and Haddad arrive. Winslow quickly flies to place the Pearl in its box and then sits on a passing cloud watching the Villagers greet Haddad. A scurrying commences, and the entire village gathers to hear Haddad tell of his trek. They cheer to hear the Black Pearl has been found. The Elders lead the villagers to see the Black Pearl safely nested in its home.

EVERY NIGHT WINSLOW TAKES THE PEARL FROM ITS BOX AND WARMS IT IN HIS POUCH. One morning the skin is red and glowing hot. Winslow puts the Pearl back in its box and moves speedily to wake Haddad. With much hugging they say good-bye. Haddad races to the Pearl. The skin has opened and out pours a myriad of new little pearls, all colors, shining and glowing. The new Pearls roll into the village and beyond. The Villagers are momentarily speechless by the sight of hundreds of pearls rolling through their lanes. They are shocked into telling the stories that had created friction and animosity among them. The Elders collect all the tales. The work of healing begins. This ends the tale of Braughn—but inside each new pearl is the seed of a Black Pearl waiting to be called for a new journey. Seek your own Black Pearl.